HE CAN WHO THINKS HE CAN

Orison Swett Marden

HAWK PRESS

Published by

Hawk Press

4836/24, Ansari Road, Daryaganj
New Delhi – 110 002
Phones : 9643330713, 91-11-23278618, 91-11-35676207
E-mail: thehawkpress@gmail.com
www.thehawkpress.com

ISBN: 978-93-88841-08-5

CONTENTS

I.

HE CAN WHO THINKS HE CAN

I PROMISED my God I would do it." In September, 1862, when Lincoln issued his preliminary emancipation proclamation, the sublimest act of the nineteenth century, he made this entry in his diary. I promised my God I would do it." Does any one doubt that such a mighty resolution added power to this marvelous man; or that it nerved him to accomplish what he had undertaken? Neither ridicule nor caricature neither dread of enemies nor desertion of friends, could shake his indomitable faith in his ability to lead the nation through the greatest struggle in its history.

Napoleon, Bismarck, and all other great achievers had colossal faith in themselves. It doubled, trebled, or even quadrupled the ordinary power of these men. In no other way can we account for the achievements of Luther, Wesley, or Savonarola. Without this sublime faith, this confidence in her mission, how could the simple country maiden, Jeanne d'Arc, have led and controlled the French army? This divine self-confidence multiplied her power a thousandfold, until even the king obeyed her, and she led his stalwart troops as if they were children.

After William Pitt was dismissed from office, he said to the Duke of Devonshire," I am sure I can save this country, and that no-body else can." "For eleven weeks," says Bancroft, "England was without a minister. At length the king and aristocracy recognized Pitt's ascendency, and yielded to him the reins."

It was his unbounded confidence in his ability that compelled the recognition and led to the supremacy in England of Benjamin

Disraeli, the once despised Jew. He did not quail or lose heart when the hisses and jeers of the British parliament rang in his ears. He sat down amid the jeering members, saying," You will yet hear me." He felt within him then the confidence of power that made him prime minister of England, and turned sneers and hisses into admiration and applause.

Much of President Roosevelt's success has been due to his colossal self-confidence. He believes in Roosevelt, as Napoleon believed in Napoleon. There is nothing timid or half-hearted about our great president. He goes at everything with that gigantic assurance, with that tremendous confidence, which half wins the battle before he begins. It is astonishing how the world makes way for a resolute soul, and how obstacles get out of the path of a determined man who believes in himself. There is no philosophy by which a man can do a thing when he thinks he can't. What can defeat a strong man who believes in himself and cannot be ridiculed down, talked down, or written down? Poverty cannot dishearten him, misfortune deter him, or hardship turn him a hair's breadth from his course. Whatever comes, he keeps his eye on the goal and pushes ahead.

What would you think of a young man, ambitious to become a lawyer, who should surround himself with a medical atmosphere and spend his time reading medical books? Do you think he would ever become a great lawyer by following such a course? No, he must put himself in a law atmosphere; go where he can absorb it and be steeped in it until he is attuned to the legal note. He must be so grafted upon the legal tree that he can feel its sap circulating through him.

How long will it take a young man to become successful who puts himself in an atmosphere of failure and remains in it until he is soaked, saturated, with the idea? How long will it take a man who depreciates himself, talks failure, thinks failure, walkslike a failure and dresses like a failure; who is always complaining of the insurmountable difficulties in his way, and whose every step is on the road to failure how long will it take him to arrive at the success goal? Will anyone believe in him or expect him to win?

The majority of failures began to deteriorate by doubting or depreciating themselves, or by losing confidence in their own ability. The moment you harbor doubt and begin to lose faith in yourself, you capitulate to the enemy. Every time you acknowledge weakness, inefficiency, or lack of ability, you weaken your self-confidence, and that is to undermine the very foundation of all achievement.

So long as you carry around a failure atmosphere, and radiate doubt and discouragement, you will be a failure. Turn about face; cut off all the currents of failure thoughts, of discouraged thoughts. Boldly face your goal with a stout heart and a determined endeavor and you will find that things will change for you; but you must see a new world before you can live in it. It is to what you see, to what you believe, to what you struggle incessantly to attain, that you will approximate.

"Trust thyself ; every heart vibrates to that iron string."

I know people who have been hunting for months for a situation, because they go into an office with a confession of weakness in their very manner; they show their lack of self-confidence. Their prophecy of failure is in their face, in their bearing. They surrender before the battle begins. They are living witnesses against themselves.

When you ask a man to give you a position, and he reads this language in your face and manner, "Please give me a position ; do not kick me out; fate is against me; I am an unlucky dog; I am disheartened; I have lost confidence in myself," he will only have contempt for you ; he will say to himself that you are not a man, to start with, and he will get rid of you as soon as he can.

If you expect to get a position, you must go into an office with the air of a conqueror; you must fling out confidence from yourself before you can convince an employer that you are the man he is looking for. You must show by your very presence that you are a man of force, a man who can do things with vigor, cheerfulness, and enthusiasm.

Self-reliance which carries great, vigorous self-faith has ever been the best substitute for friends, pedigree, influence, and money. It is the best capital in the world; it has mastered more obstacles, overcome more difficulties, and carried through more enterprises than any other human quality.

I have interviewed many timid people as to why they let opportunities pass by them that were eagerly seized by others with much less ability, and the answer was invariably a confession like the following: "I have not courage," said one; "I lack confidence in myself," said another ; " I shrink from trying for fear I shall make a mistake and have the mortification of being turned down," said a third; " It would look so cheeky for me to have the nerve to put myself forward," said a fourth; " Oh, I do not think it would be right to seek a place so far above me," said another, " I think I ought to wait until the place seeks me, or I am better prepared." So they run through the whole gamut of self-distrust. This shrinking, this timidity or self-effacement, often proves a worse enemy to success than actual incompetence. Take the lantern in the hand, and you will always have light enough for your next step, no matter how dark, for the light will move along with you. Do not try to see a long way ahead. " One step enough for me."

A physical trainer in one of our girls' colleges says that his first step is to establish the girls in self-confidence; to lead them to think only of the ends to be attained and not of the means. He shows them that the greater power lies behind the muscles, in the mind, and points to the fact so frequently demonstrated, that a person in a supreme crisis, as in a fire or other catastrophe, can exert strength out of all proportion to his muscle. He thus helps them to get rid of fear and timidity, the great handicaps to achievement.

I believe if we had a larger conception of our possibilities, a larger faith in ourselves, we could accomplish infinitely more. And if we only better understood our divinity we would have this larger faith. We are crippled by the old orthodox idea of man's inferiority. *There is no inferiority about the man that God made. The only inferiority in us is what we put into ourselves. What God made is perfect*. The trouble is that most of us are but a burlesque of the man God patioterned and intended. A Harvard graduate, who has been out of college a number of years, writes that because of his lack of self-confidence he has never earned more than twelve dollars a week. A graduate of Princeton tells us that, except for a brief period, he has never been able to earn more than a dollar a day. These men do not dare to assume responsibility. Their timidity and want of faith in themselves destroy their efficiency. The great trouble with many of us is that we do not believe enough in ourselves. We do not realize our power. Man was made to hold up his head and carry himself like a conqueror, not like a slave, as a success, not as a failure, to assert his God-given birthright. *Self-depreciation is a crime.*

If you would be superior, you must hold the thought of superiority constantly in the mind. A singularly modest man of so retiring a disposition that at one time he did not show half of his great ability, whose shrinking nature and real talent for self-abasement had actually given him an inferior appearance, told me one day how he had counteracted this tendency toward self-depreciation. Among other things, he said he had derived great benefit from the practice he had formed of going about the streets, especially where he was not known, with an air of great importance, as though imagining himself the mayor of the city, the governor of the state, or even the President of the United States. By merely looking as though he expected everybody to recognize that he must be a person of note, he changed not only his appearance, but also his convictions. It raised him immeasurably in his own estimation. It had a marked effect upon his whole character. Where he once walked through the streets shrinking from the gaze of others and dreading their scrutiny, he now boldly invites, even demands, attention by his evident supeiority, for he has the appearance of one whom people would like to know. In other words, he has caught a glimpse of his divinity; he really feels his superiority, and his self-respecting manner reflects it.

Be sure that your success will never rise higher than your confidence in yourself. The greatest artist in the world could not paint the face of a madonna with a model of depravity in his mind. You cannot succeed while doubting yourself or thinking thoughts of failure. Cling to success thoughts. Fill your mind with cheerful, optimistic pictures, pictures of achievement. This will scatter the spectres of doubt and fear and send a power through you which will transform) you into an achiever. No matter how poor or how hemmed in you may be, stoutly deny the power of adversity or poverty to keep you down. Constantly assert your superiority to environment. Believe in yourself; feel that you are to dominate your surroundings. Resolve that you will be the master and not the slave of circumstances. This very assertion of superiority; this assumption of power; this affirmation of your ability to succeed, the attitude that claims success as an inalienable birthright, will strengthen the whole man and give great added power to the combination of faculties which doubt, fear and lack of confidence undermine.

Self-confidence marshals all one's faculties and twists their united strength into one mighty achievement cable. It carries conviction. It makes other people believe in us. What has not been accomplished through its miraculous power! What triumphs in invention, in art, and in discovery have been wrought through its magic! What does not civilization owe to the invincible self-faith of its inventors, its discoverers, its railroad builders, its mine developers and city builders? It has won a thousand victories in science and in war which were deemed impossible by faint-hearted doubters.

The fact that you believe implicitly that you can do what may seem impossible or very difficult to others, shows that there is something within you that has gotten a glimpse of power sufficient to do the thing.

Many men who have achieved great things cannot account for their faith. They cannot tell why they had the implicit confidence that they could do what they undertook, but the result was evidence that something within them had gotten a glimpse of latent resourcefulness, reserve power, and possibilities which would warrant that faith; and they have gone ahead often when they could not see a ray of light with implicit confidence that they would come out all right, because this faith told them so.

It told them so because it had been in communication with something within them that was divine, that which had passed the bounds of the limited and had entered the domain of the limitless.

When we begin to exercise the faculties of self-faith, self-confidence, we are stimulating and increasing the strength of the very faculties which enable us to do the thing we have set our heart on. The very exercise of faith helps us to do what we undertake, because our greater concentration develops that portion of the brain which enables us to accomplish it.

Men who have left their mark on the world have often been implicit followers of their faith when they could see no light, and their faith has led them through the wilderness of doubt and hardship into the promised land. Our faith often tells us that we may proceed safely even in the dark, when we see no light ahead. Faith is a divine leader which never misdirects us. We must only be sure that it is faith, and not merely egotism or selfish desire.

Our faith puts us in touch with the infinite; opens the way to unbounded possibilities, limitless power. It is the truth of our being. It is the one thing that we can be sure will not mislead us.

An unwavering belief in oneself destroys the greatest enemies of fear, doubt, and vacillation. It removes the thousand and one obstacles which impede the progress of the weak and irresolute. Faith in one's mission in the conviction that the Creator has given us power to realize our life call, as it is written in our blood and stamped on our brain cells, is the secret of all power.

Poverty and failure are self-invited. The disasters people dread often come to them. Worry and anxiety enfeeble their force of mind and so blunt their creative and productive faculties that they are unable to exercise them properly. Fear of failure, or lack of faith in one's ability, is one of the most potent causes of failure. Many people of splendid powers have attained only mediocre success, and some are total failures, because they set bounds to their achievement, beyond which they did not allow themselves to think that they could pass. They put limitations to their ability; they cast stumbling blocks in their way by aiming only at mediocrity or predicting failure for themselves, talking their wares down instead of up, disparaging their business, and belittling their powers.

Thoughts are forces, and the constant affirmation of one's inherent right and power to succeed will change inhospitable conditions and unkind environments to favorable ones. If you resolve upon success with energy, you will very soon create a success atmosphere and things will come your way. *You can make, yourself a success magnet.*

"If things would only change!" you cry. What is it that changes things? Wishing, or hustling? dreaming, or working? Can you expect them to change while you merely sit down and wish them to change? How long would it take you to build a house sitting on the foundation and wishing that it would go up? Wishing does not amount to anything unless it is backed by endeavor, determination, and grit.

Webster's father was much chagrined and pained when Daniel refused a fifteen-hundred-dollar clerkship in the court of common pleas in New Hampshire, which he had worked hard to secure for him after he left college. "Daniel," he said, "don't you mean to take that office?" "No, indeed, father; I hope I can do much better than that. I mean to use my tongue in the courts, not my pen. I mean to be an actor, not a register of other men's acts." Sublime self-faith was characteristic of this giant's career.

Every child should be taught to expect success, and to believe that he was born to achieve, as the acorn is destined to become an oak. It is cruel for parents and teachers to tell children that they are dull or stupid, or that they are not like others of their age. They should inspire them, instead, with hope and confidence and belief in their success birthright. A child should be trained to expect great things, and should believe firmly in his God-given power to accomplish something worth while in the world.

Without self-faith and an iron will man is but the plaything of chance, a puppet of circumstances. With these he is a king, and it is in childhood the seeds must be sown that will make him a conqueror in life.

If you want to reach nobility, you can never do it by holding the thought of inferiority, the thought that you are not as good as other people; that you are not as able; that you cannot do this; that you cannot do that. "Can't" philosophy never does anything but tear down; it never builds up. If you want to amount to anything in the world, you must hold up your head. Say to yourself continually: "I am no beggar. I am no pauper. I am not a failure. I am a prince. I am a king. Success is my birthright, and nobody shall deprive me of it."

A proper self-esteem is not a vulgar quality. It is a very sacred one. To esteem oneself justly is to get a glimpse of the Infinite's plan in us. It is to get the perfect image which the Creator had in mind when He formed us, the complete man or woman, not the dwarfed, pinched one which lack of self-esteem or of self-confidence sees. When we get a glimpse of our immortal selves, we shall see possibilities of which we never before dreamed. A sense of wholeness of power and self-confidence, will come into our lives which will transform them When we rate ourselves properly we shall be in tune with the Infinite; our faculties will be connected with an electric wire which carries unlimited power; and we shall no longer stumble in darkness, doubt and weakness. We shall be invincible.

II.

GETTING AROUSED

HOW'S the boy gittin' on, Davis?" asked Farmer John Field, as he watched his son, Marshall, waiting upon a customer. "Well, John, you and I are old friends," replied Deacon Davis, as he took an apple from a barrel and handed it to Marshall's father as a peace offering; " we are old friends, and I don't want to hurt your feeling's; but I'm a blunt man, and air going' to tell you the truth. Marshall is a good, steady boy, all right, but he wouldn't make a merchant if he stayed in my store a thousand years. He weren't cut out for a merchant. Take him back to the farm, John, and teach him how to milk cows !"

If Marshall Field had remained as clerk in Deacon Davis's store in Pittsfield, Massachusetts, where he got his first position, he could never have become one of the world's merchant princes. But when he went to Chicago and saw the marvelous examples around him of poor boys who had won success, it aroused his ambition and fired him with the determination to be a great merchant himself. "If others can do such wonderful things," he asked himself," why cannot I ?

"Of course, there was the making of a great merchant in Mr. Field from the start; but circumstances, an ambition-arousing environment, had a great deal to do with stimulating his latent energy and bringing out his reserve force. It is doubtful if he would have climbed so rapidly in any other place than Chicago. In 1856, when young Field went there, this marvelous city was just starting on its unparalleled career. It had then only about eighty five thousand inhabitants. A few years before it had been a mere Indian trading village. But the city grew by leaps and bounds, and always beat the predictions of its most sanguine inhabitants. Success was in the air. Everybody felt that there were great possibilities there.

Many people seem to think that ambition is a quality born within us; that it is not susceptible to improvement; that it is something thrust upon us which will take care of itself. But it is a passion that responds very quickly to cultivation, and it requires constant care and education, just as the faculty for music or art does, or it will atrophy.

If we do not try to realize our ambition, it will not keep sharp and defined. Our faculties become dull and soon lose their power if they are not exercised. How can we expect our ambition to remain fresh and vigorous through years of inactivity, indolence, or indifference? If we constantly allow opportunities to slip by us without making any attempt to grasp them, our inclination will grow duller and weaker. "

What I most need," as Emerson says, " is somebody to make me do what I can." To do what I can, that is my problem; not what a Napoleon or a Lincoln could do, but what I can do. It makes all the difference in the world to me whether I bring out the best thing in me or the worst, whether I utilize ten, fifteen, twenty-five, or ninety per cent, of my ability.

Everywhere we see people who have reached middle life or later without being aroused. They have developed only a small percentage of their success possibilities. They are still in a dormant state. The best thing in them lies so deep that it has never been awakened. When we meet these people we feel conscious that they have a great deal of latent power that has never been exercised. Great possibilities of usefulness and of achievement are, all unconsciously, going to waste within them.

Some time ago there appeared in the news-papers an account of a girl who had reached the age of fifteen years, and yet had only attained the mental development of a small child. Only a few things interested her. She was dreamy, inactive, and indifferent to everything around her most of the time until, one day, while listening to a hand organ on the street, she suddenly awakened to full consciousness. She came to herself; her faculties were aroused, and in a few days she leaped forward years in her development. Almost in a day she passed from childhood to budding womanhood. Most of us have an enormous amount of power, of latent force, slumbering within us, as it slumbered in this girl, which could do marvels if we would only awaken it.

The judge of the municipal court in a flourishing western city, one of the most highly esteemed jurists in his state, was in middle life, before his latent power was aroused, an ill-literate blacksmith. He is now sixty, the owner of the finest library in his city, with the reputation of being its best-read man, and one whose highest endeavor is to help his fellow man. What caused the revolution in his life? The hearing of a single lecture on the value of education. This was what stirred the slumbering power within him, awakened his ambition, and set his feet in the path of self-development.

I have known several men who never realized their possibilities until they reached middle life. Then they were suddenly aroused, as if from a long sleep, by reading some inspiring, stimulating book, by listening to a sermon or a lecture, or by meeting some friend, someone with high ideals, who understood, believed in, and encouraged them.

It will make all the difference in the world to you whether you are with people who are watching for ability in you, people who believe in, encourage, and praise you, or whether you are with those who are forever breaking your idols, blasting your hopes, and throwing cold water on your aspirations.

The chief probation officer of the children's court in New York, in his report for 1905, says: " Removing a boy or girl from improper environment is the first step in his or her reclamation." The New York Society for the Prevention of Cruelty to Children, after thirty years of investigation of cases involving the social and moral welfare of over half a million of children, has also come to the conclusion that environment is stronger than heredity.

Even the strongest of us are not beyond the reach of our environment. No matter how independent, strong-willed, and determined our nature, we are constantly being modified by our surroundings. Take the best-born child, with the greatest inherited advantages, and let it be reared by savages, and how many of its inherited tendencies will remain? If brought up from infancy in a barbarous, brutal atmosphere, it will, of course, become brutal. The story is told of a well-born child who, being lost or abandoned as an infant, was suckled by a wolf with her own young ones, and who actually took on all the characteristics of the wolf, walked on all fours, howled like a wolf, and ate like one.

It does not take much to determine the lives of most of us. We naturally follow the examples about us, and, as a rule, we rise or fall according to the strongest current in which we live. The poet's " I am a part of all that I have met " is not a mere poetic flight of fancy; it is an absolute truth. Everything every sermon or lecture or conversation you have heard, every person who has touched your life has left an impress upon your character, and you are never quite the same person after the association or experience. You are a little different, modified somewhat from what you were before, just as Beecher was never the same man after reading Ruskin.

Some years ago a party of Russian workmen were sent to this country by a Russian firm of shipbuilders, in order that they might acquire American methods and catch the American spirit. Within six months the Russians had become almost the equals of the American artisans among whom they worked. They had developed ambition, individuality, personal initiative, and a marked degree of excellence in their work. A year after their return to their own country, the deadening, non-progressive atmosphere about them had done its work. The men had lost the desire to improve; they were again plodders, with no goal beyond the day's work. The ambition aroused by stimulating environment had sunk to sleep again.

Our Indian schools sometimes publish, by side, photographs of the Indian youths as they come from the reservation and as they look when they are graduated, well dressed, intelligent, with the fire of ambition in their eyes. We predict great things for them; but the majority of those who go back to their tribes, after struggling awhile to keep up their new standards, gradually drop back to their old manner of living. There are, of course, many notable exceptions, but these are strong characters, able to resist the downward-dragging tendencies about them.

If you interview the great army of failures, you will find that multitudes have failed because they never got into a stimulating, encouraging environment, because their ambition was never aroused, or because they were not strong enough to rally under depressing, discouraging, or vicious surroundings. Most of the people we find in prisons and poor-houses are pitiable examples of the influence of an environment which appealed to the worst instead of to the best in them.

Whatever you do in life, make any sacrifice necessary to keep in an ambition-arousing atmosphere, an environment that will stimulate you to self-development. Keep close to people who understand you, who believe in you, who will help you to discover yourself and encourage you to make the most of yourself. This may make all the difference to you between a grand success and a mediocre existence. Stick to those who are trying to do something and to be somebody in the world, people of 'high aims, lofty ambition. Keep close to those who are dead-in-earnest. Ambition is contagious. You will catch the spirit that dominates in your environment. The success of those about you who are trying to climb upward will encourage and stimulate you to struggle harder if you have not done quite so well yourself.

There is a great power in a battery of individuals who are struggling for the achievement of high aims, a great magnetic force which will help you to attract the object of your ambition. It is very stimulating to be with people whose aspirations run parallel with your own. If you lack energy, if you are naturally lazy, indolent, or inclined to take it easy, you will be urged forward by the constant prodding of the more ambitious.

III.

EDUCATION BY ABSORPTION

JOHN WANAMAKER was once asked to invest in an expedition to recover from the Spanish Main doubloons which for half a century had lain at the bottom of the sea in sunken frigates.

" Young men, he replied, " I know of a better expedition than this, right here. Near your own feet lie treasures untold; you can have them all by faithful study.

" Let us not be content to mine the most coal, to make the largest locomotives, to weave the largest quantities of carpets ; but, amid the sounds of the pick, the blows of the hammer, the rattle of the looms, and the roar of the machinery, take care that the immortal mechanism of God's own hand the mind is still full-trained for the highest and noblest service.

" The uneducated man is always placed at a great disadvantage. No matter how much natural ability one may have, if he is ignorant, he is discounted. It is not enough to possess ability, it must be made available by mental discipline.

We ought to be ashamed to remaining ignorance in a land where the blind, the deaf and dumb, and even cripples and invalids, manage to obtain a good education.

Many youths throw away little opportunities for self-culture because they cannot see great ones. They let the years slip by without any special effort at self-improvement, until they are shocked in middle life, or later, by waking up to the fact that they are still ignorant of what they ought to know.

Everywhere we go we see men and women, especially from twenty-five to forty years of age, who are cramped and seriously handicapped by the lack of early training. I often get letters from such people, asking if it is possible for them to educate themselves so late in life. Of course it is. There are so many good correspondence schools today, and institutions like Chautauqua, so many evening schools, lectures, books, libraries, and periodicals, that men and women who are determined to improve themselves have abundant opportunities to do so.

While you lament the lack of an early education and think it too late to begin, you may be sure that there are other young men and young women not very far from you who are making great strides in self-improvement, though they may not have half as good an opportunity for it as you have.

The first thing to do is to make a resolution, strong, vigorous, and determined, that you are going to be an educated man or woman; that you are not going to go through life humiliated by ignorance; that, if you have been deprived of early advantages, you are going to make up for their loss. Resolve that you will no longer be handicapped and placed at a disadvantage for that which you can remedy.

You will find the whole world will change to you when you change your attitude toward it. You will be surprised to see how quickly you can very materially improve your mind after you have made a vigorous resolve to do so. Go about it with the same determination that you would to make money or to learn a trade. There is a divine hunger in every normal being for self-expansion, a yearning for growth or enlargement. Beware of stifling this craving of nature for self-unfoldment.

Man was made for growth. It is the object, the explanation, of his being. To have an ambition to grow larger and broader every day, to push the horizon of ignorance a little further away, to become a little richer in knowledge, a little wiser, and more of a man that is an ambition worth while. It is not absolutely necessary that an education should be crowded into a few years of school life. The best-educated people are those who are always learning, always absorbing knowledge from every possible source and at every opportunity.

I know young people who have acquired a better education, a

finer culture, through a habit of observation, or of carrying a book in the pocket to read at odd moments, or by taking courses in correspondence schools, than many who have gone through college. Youths who are quick to catch at new ideas, and who are in frequent contact with superior minds, not only often acquire a personal charm, but even, to a remarkable degree, develop mental power.

The world is a great university. From the cradle to the grave we are always in God's great kindergarten, where everything is trying to teach us its lesson; to give us its great secret. Some people are always at school, always storing up precious bits of knowledge. Everything has a reason for them. It all depends upon the eye that can see, the mind that can appropriate.

Very few people ever learn how to use their eyes. They go through the world with a superficial glance at things; their eye pictures are so faint and so dim that details are lost and no strong impression is made on the mind. Yet the eye was intended for a great educator. The brain is a prisoner, never getting out to the outside world. It depends upon its five or six servants, the senses, to bring it material, and the larger part of it comes through the eye. The man who has learned the art of seeing things looks with his brain.

I know a father who is training his boy to develop his powers of observation. He will send him out upon a street with which he is not familiar for a certain length of time, and then question him on his return to see how many things he has observed. He sends him to the show windows of great stores, to museums and other public places to see how many of the objects he has seen the boy can recall and describe when he gets home. The father says that this practice develops in the boy a habit of *seeing* things, instead of merely *looking* at them.

When a new student went to the great naturalist, Professor Agassiz of Harvard, he would give him a fish and tell him to look it over for half an hour or an hour, and then describe to him what he saw. After the student thought he had told everything about the fish, the professor would say, " You have not really seen the fish yet. Look at it a while longer, and then tell me what you see." He would repeat this several times, until the student developed a capacity for observation.

If we go through life like an interrogation point, holding an alert, inquiring mind toward everything, we can acquire great mental wealth, wisdom which is beyond all material riches. Ruskin's mind was enriched by the observation of birds, insects, beasts, trees, rivers, mountains, pictures of sunset and landscape, and by memories of the song of the lark and of the brook. His brain held thousands of pictures of paintings, of architecture, of sculpture, a wealth of material which he reproduced as a joy for all time. Everything gave up its lesson, its secret, to his inquiring mind.

The habit of absorbing information of all kinds from others is of untold value. A man is weak and ineffective in proportion as he secludes himself from his kind. There is a constant stream of power, a current of forces running to and fro between individuals who come in contact with one another, if they have inquiring minds. We are all giving and taking perpetually when we associate together. The achiever today must keep in touch with the society around him; he must put his finger on the pulse of the great busy world and feel its throbbing life. He must be a part of it, or there will be some lack in his life.

A single talent which one can use effectively is worth more than ten talents imprisoned by ignorance. Education means that knowledge has been assimilated and become a part of the person. It is the ability to express the power within one, to give out what one knows, that measures efficiency and achievement. Pent-up knowledge is useless.

People who feel their lack of education, and who can afford the outlay, can make wonderful strides in a year by putting themselves under good tutors, who will direct their reading and study along different lines.

The danger of trying to educate oneself lies in desultory, disconnected, aimless studying which does not give anything like the benefit to be derived from the pursuit of a definite program for self-improvement. A person who wishes to educate himself at home should get some competent, well-trained person to lay out a plan for him, which can only be effectively done when the adviser knows the vocation, the tastes, and the needs of the would-be student. Anyone who aspires to an education, whether in country or city, can find someone to at least guide his studies; some teacher, clergyman, lawyer, or other educated person in the community to help him.

There is one special advantage in self-education, you can adapt your studies to your own particular needs better than you could in school or college. Everyone who reaches middle life without an education should first read and study along the line of his own vocation, and then broaden himself as much as possible by reading on other lines.

One can take up, alone, many studies, such as history, English literature, rhetoric, drawing, mathematics, and can also acquire by oneself, almost as effectively as with a teacher, a reading knowledge of foreign languages.

The daily storing up of valuable information for use later in life, the reading of books that will inspire and stimulate to greater endeavor, the constant effort to try to improve oneself and one's condition in the world, are worth far more than a bank account to a youth.

How many girls there are in this country who feel crippled by the fact that they have not been able to go to college. And yet they have the time and the material close at hand for obtaining a splendid education, but they waste their talents and opportunities in frivolous amusements and things which do not count in forceful character-building.

It is not such a very great undertaking to get all the essentials of a college course at home, or at least a fair substitute for it. Every hour in which one focuses his mind vigorously upon his studies at home may be as beneficial as the same time spent in college.

Every well-ordered household ought to protect the time of those who desire to study at home. At a fixed hour every evening during the long winter there should be by common consent a quiet period for mental concentration, for what is worth while in mental discipline, a quiet hour uninterrupted by time thief callers.

In thousands of homes where the members are devoted to each other, and should encourage and help each other along, it is made almost impossible for anyone to take up reading, studying, or any exercise for self-improvement. Perhaps someone is thoughtless and keeps interrupting the others so that they cannot concentrate their minds; or those who have nothing in common with your aims or your earnest life drop in to spend an evening in idle chatter. They have no ideals outside of the bread-and-butter and amusement questions, and do not realize how they are hindering you.

There is constant temptation to waste one's evenings and it takes a stout ambition and a firm resolution to separate oneself from a jolly, fun-loving, and congenial family circle, or happy-hearted youthful callers, in order to try to rise above the common herd of unambitious persons who are content to slide along, totally ignorant of everything but the requirements of their particular vocations.

A habit of forcing yourself to fix your mind steadfastly and systematically upon certain studies, even if only for periods of a few minutes at a time, is, of itself, of the greatest value. This habit helps one to utilize the odds and ends of time which are unavailable to most people because they have never been trained to concentrate the mind at regular intervals.

A good understanding of the possibilities that live in spare moments is a great success asset.

The very reputation of always trying to improve yourself, of seizing every opportunity to fit yourself for something better, the reputation of being dead-in-earnest, determined to be somebody and to do something in the world, would be of untold assistance to you. People like to help those who are trying to help themselves. They will throw opportunities in their way. Such a reputation is the best kind of capital to start with.

One trouble with people who are smarting tinder the consciousness of deficient education is that they do not realize the immense value of utilizing spare minutes. Like many boys who will not save their pennies and small change because they cannot see how a fortune could ever grow by the saving, they cannot see how a little studying here and there each day will ever amount to a good substitute for i a college education.

I know a young man who never even attended a high school, and yet educated himself so superbly that he has been offered a professorship in a college. Most of his knowledge was gained during his odds and ends of time, while working hard at his vocation. Spare time meant something to him.

The correspondence schools deserve very great credit for inducing hundreds of thousands of people, including clerks, mill operatives, and employees of all kinds, to take their courses, and thus save for study the odds and ends of time which otherwise would probably be thrown away. We have heard of some most remarkable instances of rapid advancement which these correspondence school students have made by reason of the improvement in their education. Many students have reaped a thousand per cent, on their educational investment. It has saved them years of drudgery and has shortened wonderfully the road to their goal.

Wisdom will not open her doors to those who are not willing to pay the price in self-sacrifice, in hard work. Her jewels are too precious to scatter before the idle, the ambitionless.

The very resolution to redeem yourself from ignorance at any cost is the first great step toward gaining an education.

Charles Wagner once wrote to an American regarding his little boy," May he know the price of the hours. God bless the rising boy who will do his best, for never losing a bit of the precious and God-given time."

There is untold wealth locked up in the long winter evenings and odd moments ahead of you. A great opportunity confronts you. What will you do with it ?

IV.

FREEDOM AT ANY COST

WERE you to decide to risk your reputation, your material welfare, your whole future, upon some great physical or mental contest which should extend over a considerable period of time, you would begin long beforehand to train or discipline yourself for the decisive conflict. You would not, if possible to avoid doing so, go into it handicapped.

Every person who is ambitious to make his life count, to do what is worth while, is entering upon just such a contest. In starting upon a conflict so grave, so significant, and which affects the whole future, the first thing to do is to get absolute freedom from everything which strangles ambition, discourages effort, and hinders progress; freedom from everything which saps vitality, enslaves the faculties, and wastes energy; to remove every obstruction from the way and leave a clear path to one's goal.

No matter how ambitious a runner may be to win, if he does not train off his surplus fat, if he is hampered with extra clothing, or runs with feet cramped and sore, his race is lost.

The trouble with most of us is that, while ambitious to succeed, we do not put ourselves in a condition to win; we do not cut the cords which bind us, or try to get rid of the entanglements and obstructions that hinder us. We trust too much to luck.

To eliminate everything that can possibly retard us, to get into as harmonious an environment as possible, is the first preparation for a successful career. There are tens of thousands of people who have ability and inclination to rise out of mediocrity, and to do something worth while in the world, but who never do so because they cannot break the chains that bind their movements. Most of us are so bound in some part of our nature that we cannot get free; cannot gain the liberty to do the larger thing possible to us. We go through life doing the smaller, the meaner, when the larger, the grander would be possible could we get rid of the things that handicap us.

Every normal man has a reserve power within him, a mighty coil of force and purpose, which would enable him to make his life strong and complete, were he free to express the largest and the best things in him, were he not fettered by some bond, physical or moral.

You can tie a strong horse with a very small cord, and he cannot show his greatest speed or strength till he is free. On every hand we see people with splendid ability tied down by some apparently insignificant thing which handicaps all their movements. They cannot go ahead until they are free. A giant would be a weakling if he were confined in so small a space that he did not have room to exert himself with freedom.

The majority of people live in a cramped and uncongenial environment; in an atmosphere which dampens enthusiasm, discourages ambition and effort, scatters energy, and wastes time. They have not the courage or stamina to cut the shackles that bind them, to throw away, all crutches and props, and to rely on themselves to get into an environment where they can do what they desire. Their ambition finally dies through discouragement and inaction.

I recall the case of a youth with artistic talent who let precious years go by, drifting by accident from one vocation to another, without encouraging this God-given ability or making any great effort to get rid of the little things which stood in the way of a great career, although he was always haunted by a longing for it. He was conscientious in his everyday work, but his heart was never in it. His artistic nature yearned for expression; to get away from the work against which every faculty protested, and to go abroad and study; but he was poor, and, although his work was drudgery and his whole soul loathed it, he was afraid of the hardships and the obstacles he would have to encounter if he answered the call that ran in his blood. He kept resolving to break away and to follow the promptings of his ambition, but he also kept waiting and waiting for a more favorable opportunity, until, after a number of years, he found other things crowding into his life. His longing for art became fainter and fainter; the call was less and less imperative. Now he rarely speaks of his early aspirations, for his ambition is practically dead. Those who know him feel that something grand and sacred has gone out of him, and that, although he has been industrious and honest, he has never expressed the real meaning of his life, the highest thing in him.

I know a woman who in her youth and early womanhood had marked musical ability a voice rich, powerful, sympathetic. She had also a beautiful face and a magnetic personality. Nature had been very generous to her and she longed to express her remarkable powers, but she was in a most discouraging environment. Her family did not understand her or sympathize with her ambition; and she finally became accustomed to her shackles and, like a prisoner, ceased to struggle for freedom. A songstress of international fame who heard her voice said that she had it in her to make one of the world's greatest singers. But she yielded to the wishes of her parents and the fascinations of society until the ambition gradually died out of her life. She says that the dying of this great passion was indescribably painful. She settled down to the duties of a wife, but has never been really happy, and has always carried in her face an absent, far-away look of disappointment. Her unused talent was a great loss to the world, and a loss indescribable to herself. She drags out a dissatisfied existence, always regretting the past, and vainly wishing, that, instead of letting her ambition die, she had struggled to realize it.

Timidity also hinders freedom. Thousands of able young men and young women in this country are ambitious to make the most of themselves, but are completely fettered or held back by an abnormal timidity, a lack of selffaith. They feel great unused powers within struggling for expression, but dread that they may fail. The fear of being thought forward or egotistical seals their lips, palsies their hands, and drives their ambition back upon itself to die of inaction. They do not dare to give up a certainty for an uncertainty; they are afraid to push ahead. They wait and wait, hoping that some mysterious power may liberate them and give them confidence and hope.

Many people are imprisoned by ignorance. They never reach the freedom which education gives. Their mental powers are never unlocked. They have not the grit to struggle for emancipation, the stamina to make up for the lack of early training. They think they are too old to begin; the price of freedom seems too high to pay at their time of life, and so they plod upon a low plain when they could have gained the heights where superiority dwells. Others are so bound by the fetters of prejudice and superstition that their lives are narrow and mean. These are the most hopeless of all. They are so blinded that they do not even know they are not free, but they think other people are in prison.

If you would attain that largeness of life, that fulness of self-expression, which expands all the faculties, you must get freedom at any cost. Nothing will compensate you for stifling the best thing in you. Bring it out at any sacrifice. It often takes a great deal of friction, of suffering, of struggling with obstacles and misfortunes, before the true strength of one's character is brought out. The diamond could never reveal its depths of brilliancy and beauty, but for the friction of the stone which grinds its facets, polishes it, and lets in the light which discloses its hidden wealth. This is the price of its liberation from darkness.

Ask the majority of men and women who have done great things in the world, to what they owe their strength, their breadth of mind, and the diversity of experience which has enriched their lives. They will tell you that these are the fruits of struggle; that they acquired their finest discipline, their best character drill, in the effort to escape from an uncongenial environment; to break the bonds which enslaved them ; to obtain an education ; to get away from poverty; to carry out some cherished plan; to reach their ideal, whatever it was.

The efforts we are obliged to make to free ourselves from the bonds of poverty or heredity, of passion or prejudice, whatever it is that holds us back from our heart's desire, call to our aid spiritual and physical resources which would have remained forever unused, perhaps undiscovered, but for the necessity thrust upon us.

Unsatisfied longings and stifled ambitions eat away the very heart of desire. They sap strength of character, destroy hope, and blot out ideals. They play havoc with the lives of men and women, they make them mere shells, empty promises of what they might have been.

I do not believe that anybody in any circumstances can be happy until he expresses that which God has made to dominate in his life; until he has given vent to that grand passion which speaks loudest in his nature; until he has made the best use of that gift which was intended to take precedence of all his other powers.

"No man can live a half life when he has genuinely learned that it is a half life," said Phillips Brooks. After we have gained a glimpse of a life higher and better than we have been living, we must either (break the bonds that bind us and struggle towards the attainment of that which we see, or development will cease and deterioration set in. Even the longing to reach an ideal will soon die out if no effort is made to satisfy it. No one should follow a vocation, except by inevitable compulsion, which does not tend to unlock his prison-house and let out the man. No one should voluntarily remain in an environment which prevents his development. Civilization owes its greatest triumphs to the struggles of men and women to free themselves from the bonds of circumstance.

No man can live a full life while he is bound in any part of his nature. He must have freedom of thought as well as freedom of action to grow to his full height. There must be no shackles on his conscience, no Stirling of his best powers.

Be yourself. Do not lean or apologize. Few people belong to themselves. They are slaves to their creditors or to some entangling alliance. They do not do what they want to. They do what they are compelled to do, giving up their best energy to make a living, so that there is practically nothing left to make a life.

There are plenty of men today working for others, who really have more ability than their employers ; but who have been so enslaved, so entangled and faculty-bound by debt or unfortunate alliances, that they have not been able to get the freedom to express their ability.

Can anything compensate a promising young man for the loss of his freedom of action, his liberty of speech and conviction ? Can any money pay him for cringing and crawling, sneaking and apologizing throughout his life, when it is within his power to hold up his head and without wincing look the world squarely in the face ?

Never put yourself in a position, no matter what the inducement whether a big salary or other financial reward, or the promise of position or influence, where you cannot act the part of a man. Let no consideration tie your tongue or purchase your opinion. Regard your independence as your inalienable right, with which you will never part for any consideration.

One talent with freedom is infinitely better than genius tied up and entangled so that it must do everything at a disadvantage. Of what use is a giant intellect so restrained and hampered that it can only do a pygmy's work ?

To make the most of ourselves, we must cut off whatever drains vitality physical or moral and stop all the waste of life. We must cut off everything which causes friction, which tends to weaken effort, lower the ideals, and drag down the life standards; everything which tends to kill the ambition and to make us satisfied with mediocrity.

Multitudes of people, enslaved by bad physical habits, are unable to get their best selves into their work. They are kept back by a leakage of energy and vital force, resulting from bad habits and dissipation. Some are hindered by peculiarities of disposition; by stubbornness, slovenliness, meanness, revengefulness, jealousy, or envy. These are all handicaps.

Others go through life galled by their chains, but without making any serious, continuous effort to emancipate themselves. Like the elephants or other wild animals chained in the menageries, at first they rebel at their loss of freedom and try hard to break away; but gradually they become accustomed to slavery, and take it for granted that it is a necessary part of their existence.

Then, again, there are entanglements which retard the progress and nullify the efforts of many business men, such as debt, bad partners, or unfortunate social alliances. Comparatively few men belong to themselves or are really free. They go the way they are pushed. They waste a large part of their energy on that which does not really count in the main issue of life; spend their lives paying for "a dead horse," clearing up old debts that came from bad judgment, blunders, or foolish endorsements. Instead of putting on speed and gaining on life's road, they are always trying to make up for lost time. They are always in the rear never in the vanguard of their possibilities.

An ambitious young man, anxious to do what is right and eager to make a place for himself in the world, entangles himself in complications that thwart his life-purpose and cripple all his efforts; so that, no matter how hard he struggles, he is never able to get beyond mediocrity. Hopelessly in debt, with a family to support, he cannot take advantage of the great opportunities about him as he could if he were free; if he had not risked his little savings and tied up his future earnings for years ahead. His great ambition only mocks him, for he cannot satisfy it. He is tied hand and foot. Like a caged eagle, no matter how high he might soar into the ether, he must stop when he strikes the bars.

The man who trusts everybody is constantly crippling himself by entangling alliances. He indorses notes, loans money, helps everybody out, and usually gets left. He ties up his productive ability and hampers his work by his poor judgment or lack of business sense. A most estimable man of my acquaintance was ruined financially by indorsements and loans which would have been foolish even for a boy of fifteen. For many years it took every dollar he could spare from the absolute necessities of his family to pay these obligations.

Our judgment was intended to preside over our mental faculties and to help us discriminate between the wise and the foolish. That man wins who keeps a level head and uses sound judgment in every transaction.

Whatever you do, do not get involved. Make it a life rule to keep yourself clean and clear, with everything safeguarded. Before you go into anything of importance think it through to the end; make reasonably sure that you know where you are coming out. Do not risk a competence, or your home and your little savings, in the hope of getting something for nothing. Do not be carried away by the reports of those who in some venture have made a great deal on a little money, Where one makes, a hundred lose. There is no greater delusion in the world than thinking that by putting out a little " flyer " here and there you can make a few hundreds or a few thousands.

If you cannot make money in the vocation which you have chosen for your life-work, and in which you have become expert ; if you cannot get rich in the business whose every detail you understand; how can you expect that somebody else will take your money and give you a tremendous return for it, when it will not get your personal supervision ?

I know a lawyer in New York, now a millionaire (who had worked most of his way through college, and came to the metropolis an utter stranger, taking a little desk room in a broker's office near Wall street) who, at the outset, made a cast-iron rule that he would always keep himself free from debt and entangling alliances. By this inflexible rule, it is true, he often lost opportunities which would have brought him excellent returns, but he has never tied himself up in any transaction. The result is that he has not worried himself to death, but has reserved his strength. Nearly every enterprise he has gone into has been very successful, because he has not touched anything unless he could see through to the end and knew how he would come out (even taking into consideration possible shrinkage, accident, and loss). In this way, although he has never made any very brilliant strides or "lucky hits," and has not gone up by leaps and bounds, he has never had to undo what he has done, and has always kept in a sure position. He has gained the confidence not only of men in his profession, but also of capitalists and men of wealth, who have entrusted large sums to him because he has always kept his head level, and himself free from entanglements. People know that their business and their capital will be safe in his hands. Through steady growth and persistent pushing of practical certainties, he has not only become a millionaire, but a broad, progressive, comprehensive man of affairs. Develop your judgment early and exercise your caution until it becomes reliable. Your judgment is your best friend; your common sense is your great life partner, given you for guidance and to protect your interests. Depend upon these three great friends sound judgment, caution, and common sense and you will not be flung about at the mercy of adverse winds.

V.

WHAT THE WORLD OWES TO DREAMERS

ONCE when Emerson was in the company of men of affairs, who had been discussing railroads, stocks, and other business matters for some time, he said, " Gentlemen, now let us discuss real things for a while."

Emerson was called " the dreamer of dreams," because he had the prophetic vision that saw the world to be, the higher civilization to come. Tens of thousands of men and women stand to-day where he then stood almost alone.

Edison is a dreamer because he sees people half a century hence using and enjoying inventions, discoveries, and facilities which make the most advanced utilities of to-day seem very antiquated. His mind's eye sees as curiosities in museums, fifty years hence, those mechanisms and devices which now seem so marvelous to us. Dreamers in this sense are true prophets. They see the civilization that will be, long before it arrives.

As it was the dreamers of '49 who built the old San Francisco and made it the greatest port on the Western coast; so after the recent great earthquake and fire, when the city lay in ashes and three hundred thousand people were homeless, it was the dreamers of today who saw the new city in the ashes where others saw only desolation, and who, with indomitable grit, and the unconquerable American will that characterized the pioneers of a half-century before, began to plan a restored city greater and grander than the old. It was in dreams that the projectors of the great transcontinental railroads first saw teeming cities and vast business enterprises where the more "practical men, without imagination, saw only the great American desert, vast alkali plains, sage grass, and impassable mountains. The dreams of men like Collis P. Huntington and Leland Stanford bound together the East and the West with bands of steel, made the two oceans neighbors, reclaimed the desert, and built cities where before only desolation reigned.

It was the persistency and grit of dreamers that triumphed over the congressmen without imagination who advised importing dromedaries to carry the mails across the great American desert; because they said it was ridiculous, a foolish waste of money, to build a railroad to the Pacific Ocean, as there was nothing there to support a population.

It was such dreamers as those who saw the great metropolis of Chicago in a straggling Indian village; who saw Omaha, Kansas City, Denver, Salt Lake City, Los Angeles, and San Francisco many years before they arrived, that made their existence possible.

It was such dreamers as Marshall Field, Joseph Leiter, and Potter Palmer, who saw in the ashes of the burned Chicago a new and glorified city, infinitely greater and grander than the old.

Take the dreamers out of the world's history, and who would care to read it? Our dreamers! They are the advance guard of humanity ; the toilers who, with bent back and sweating brow, cut smooth roads over which man marches forward from generation to generation.

Most of the things which make life worth living, which have emancipated man from drudgery and lifted him above commonness and ugliness the great amenities of life we owe to our dreamers. The present is but the sum total of the dreams of the ages that have gone before, the dreams of the past made real. Our great ocean liners, our marvelous tunnels, our magnificent bridges, our schools, our universities, our hospitals, our libraries, our cosmopolitan cities, with their vast facilities, comforts, and treasures of art, are all the result of somebody's dreams.

We hear a great deal of talk about the impracticality of dreamers, of people whose heads are among the stars while their feet are on the earth; but where would civilization be to-day but for the dreamers ? We should still be riding in the stage-coach or tramping across continents. We should still cross the ocean in sailing ships, and our letters would be carried across continents by the pony express.

It cannot be done," cries the man without imagination. " It can be done, it shall be done," cries the dreamer; and he persists in his dreams through all sorts of privations, even to the point of starvation, if necessary, until his visions, his inventions, his discoveries, his ideas for the betterment of the race, are made practical realities.

What a picture the dreamer Columbus presented as he went about exposed to continual scoffs and indignities, characterized as an adventurer, the very children taught to regard him as a madman and pointing to their foreheads as he passed! He dreamed of a world beyond the seas, and, in spite of unspeakable obstacles, his vision became a glorious reality.

It was the men who, a quarter of a century ahead of their contemporaries, saw the marvelous Hoe press in the hand-press that made modern journalism possible. Without these dreamers our printing would still be done by hand. It was the men who were denounced as visionaries who practically annihilated space, and enabled us to converse and transact business with people thousands of miles away as though they were in the same building with us.

How many matter-of-fact, unimaginative men, who see only through practical eyes, would it take to replace in civilization au Edison, a Bell, or a Marconi?

The very practical people tell us that then imagination is all well enough in artists, musicians, and poets, but that it has little place in the great world of realities. Yet all leaders of men have been dreamers. Our great captains of industry, our merchant princes, have had powerful, prophetic imaginations. They had faith in the vast commercial possibilities of our people. If it had not been for our dreamers, the American population would still be hugging the Atlantic coast.

The most practical people in the world are those who can look far into the future and see the civilization yet to be; who can see the coming man emancipated from the narrowing, hampering fetters, limitations, and superstitions of the present day; who have the ability, to foresee things to come with the power to make them realities. The dreamers have ever been those who have achieved the seemingly impossible.

Our public parks, our art galleries, our great institutions are dotted with monuments and statues which the world has built to its dreamers, those who saw visions of better things, better days for the human race.

What horrible experiences men and women have gone through in prisons and dungeons for their dreams; dreams which were destined to lift the world from savagery and emancipate man from drudgery.

The very dreams for which Galileo and other great scientists were imprisoned and persecuted were recognized as science only a few generations later. Galileo's dream gave us a new heaven and a new earth. The dreams of Confucius, of Buddha, of Socrates, have become realities in millions of human lives. Christ Himself was denounced as a dreamer, but His whole life was a prophecy, a dream of the coming man, the coming civilization. He saw beyond the burlesque of the man God intended, beyond the deformed, weak, deficient, imperfect man heredity had made, to the perfect man, the ideal man, the image of divinity.

Our visions do not mock us. They are evidences of what is to be, the fore glimpses of possible realities. The castle in the air always precedes the castle on the earth.

George Stephenson, the poor miner, dreamed of a locomotive engine that would revolutionize the traffic of the world. While working in the coal pits for sixpence a day, or patching the clothes and mending the boots of his fellow-workmen to earn a little money to attend a night school, and at the same time supporting his blind father, he continued to dream. People called him crazy. " His roaring engine will set the houses on fire with its sparks' everybody cried. " Smoke will pollute the air; " carriage makers and coachmen will starve for want of work." See this dreamer in the House of Commons, when members of Parliament were cross-questioning him. " What," said one member, " can be more palpably absurd and ridiculous than the prospect held out of locomotives traveling twice as fast as horses? We should as soon expect the people of Woolwich to suffer themselves to be fired off upon one of Congreve's rockets, as to trust themselves to the mercy of such a machine, going at such a rate. We trust that Parliament will, in all the railways it may grant, limit the speed to eight or nine miles an hour, which is as great as can be ventured upon." But, in spite of calumny, ridicule, and opposition, this " crazy visionary" toiled on for fifteen years for the realization of his vision.

On the fourth of August, 1907, New York celebrated the centennial of the dream of Robert Fulton. See the crowd of curious scoffers at the wharves of the Hudson River at noon on Friday, August 4, 1807, to witness the results of what they thought the most ridiculous idea which ever entered a human brain ; to witness what they believed would be a most humiliating failure of the dreams of a " crank " who proposed to take a party of people up the river to Albany in a steam vessel named the " Clermont " ! " Did anybody ever hear of such an absurd idea as navigating against the current of the Hudson River without sail ? " scornfully said the scoffing wiseacres. Many of them thought that the man who had fooled away his time and money on the "Clermont" was little better than an idiot, and that he ought to be in an insane asylum. But the " Clermont " did sail up the Hudson, and Fulton was hailed as a benefactor of the human race.

What does the world not owe to Morse, who gave it its first telegraph? When the inventor asked for an appropriation of a few thousand dollars for the first experimental line from Washington to Baltimore, he was sneered at by congressmen. After discouragements which would have disheartened most men, this experimental line was completed, and some congressmen were waiting for the message which they did not believe would ever come, when one of them asked the inventor how large a package he expected to be able to send over the wire. But very quickly the message did come, and derision was changed to praise.

The dream of Cyrus W. Field, which tied two continents together by the ocean cable, was denounced as worse than folly. How long would it take to get the world's day-by-day news but for such dreamers as Field?

When William Murdock, at the close of the eighteenth century, dreamed of lighting London by means of coal gas conveyed to buildings in pipes, even Sir Humphry Davy sneeringly asked, " Do you intend taking the dome of St. Paul's for a gasometer?" Sir Walter Scott, too, ridiculed the idea of lighting London by " smoke/' but he lived to use this same smoke-dream to light his castle at Abbottsford.

"What!" said the wise scientists, " a light without a wick ? Impossible!"

How people laughed at the dreamer, Charles Goodyear, who struggled with hardships for eleven long years while trying to make india-rubber of practical use! See him in prison for debt, still dreaming, while pawning his clothes and his wife's jewelry to get a little money to keep his children from starving! Note his sublime courage and devotion to his vision even when without money to bury a dead child; while his five other children were near starvation, and his neighbors were denouncing him as insane !

Women called Ellas Howe a fool and " crank " and condemned him for neglecting his family to dream of a machine which has proved a blessing to millions of their sex.

The great masters are always idealists, seers of visions. The sculptor is a dreamer who sees the statue in the rough block before he strikes a blow with his chisel. The artist sees a vision of the finished painting in all its perfection and beauty of coloring and form before he touches a brush to the canvas.

Every palace, every beautiful structure, is first the dream of the architect. It had no previous existence in reality. The building came out of his ideal before it was made real. Sir Christopher Wren saw Saint Paul's Cathedral in all its magnificent beauty before the foundations were laid. It was his dream which revolutionized the architecture of London.

It was the dreaming Baron Haussmann who made Paris the most beautiful city in the world.

Think what we owe the beauty dreamers for making our homes and our parks so attractive ! Yet there are thousands of practical men in New York to-day who, if they could have their way, would cut Central Park up into lots and cover it with business blocks.

The achievements of every successful man are but the realized visions of his youth, his dreams of bettering his condition, of enlarging his power.

Our homes are the dreams that began with lovers and their efforts to better their condition; the dreams of those who once lived in huts and in log cabins.

The modern luxurious railway train is the dream of those who rode in the old stagecoach.

Not more than a dozen years ago the horseless carriage, the manufacture of which now promises to make one of the largest businesses in the world, was considered by most people in the same light as is the airship to-day. But there has recently been an exhibition of these " dreams "in Madison Square Garden, New York, on a scale so vast in the suggestiveness of its possibilities as to stagger credulity.

Half a dozen years since, this invention was looked upon as a mere toy, a fad for a few millionaires. Twelve years ago there was not a single factory in America making cars for the market. Fourteen years ago there were only five horseless vehicles in this country, and they had been imported at extravagant prices. To-day there are over a hundred thousand in actual use. Instead of being a toy for millionaires, the automobile is now being used in place of horses by thousands of people with ordinary incomes.

This dream is already helping us to solve the problem of crowded streets. It is proving a great educator, as well as a health giver, by tempting people into the country. The average man will ultimately, through its full realization, practically travel in his own private car. In fact this dream is becoming one of the greatest joys and blessings that has ever come to humanity.

It was the wonderful dream in steel of Carnegie, Schwab, and their associates, together with that of the elevator creator, that made the modern city with its sky-scrapers possible.

What do we not owe to our poet dreamers, who like Shakespeare, have taught us to see the uncommon in the common, the extraordinary in the ordinary?

The divinest heritage of man is the capacity to dream. It matters not how much we have to suffer to-day, if we believe there is a better to-morrow. Even " stone walls do not a prison make " to those who can dream.

Who would rob the poor of this dreaming faculty, that takes the drudgery out of their dry, dreary occupations? Who would depriven them of the luxuries which they enjoy in their dreams of a better and brighter future, of a fuller education, of more comforts for those dear to them.

There is no medicine like hope, no incentive so great and no tonic so powerful as expectation of something better to-morrow.

Dreaming is especially characteristic of the typical American. No matter how poor, or what his misfortune, he is confident, self-reliant, even defiant at fate, because he believes better days are coming. The clerk can live in a store of his own which his imagination builds. The poorest factory girl dreams of a beautiful home of her own. The humblest dream of power.

The ability to lift oneself instantly out of all perplexities, trials, troubles, and discordant environment, into an atmosphere of harmony and beauty and truth, is beyond price. How many of us would have heart enough, hope enough, and courage enough, to continue the struggle of life with enthusiasm if our power of dreaming were taken away from us?

It is this dreaming, this hoping, this constant expectancy of better things to come, that keeps up our courage, lightens our burdens, and makes clear the way.

I know a lady who has gone through the most trying and heartrending experiences for many years, and yet everybody who knows her marvels at her sweetness of temper, her balance of mind, and beauty of character. She says that she owes everything to her ability to dream; that she can at will lift herself out of the most discordant and trying conditions into a calm of absolute harmony and beauty, and come back to her work with a freshened mind and invigorated body.

The dreaming faculty, like every other faculty, may be abused. A great many people do nothing but dream. They spend all their energies in building air castles which they never try to make real; they live in an unnatural, delusive, theoretical atmosphere until the faculties become paralyzed from inaction.

It is a splendid thing to dream when you have the grit and tenacity of purpose and the resolution to match your dreams with realities, but dreaming without effort, wishing without putting forth exertion to realize the wish, undermines the character. It is only practical dreaming that counts, dreaming coupled with hard work and persistent endeavor.

Just in proportion as we make our dreams realities, shall we become strong and effective. Dreams that are realized become an inspiration for new endeavor. It is in the power to make the dream good that we find the hope of this world.

Dreaming and making good, this was what John Harvard did when with his few 'hundred dollars he made Harvard College possible. The founding of Yale College with a handful of books was but a dream made good.

President Roosevelt owes everything to his dream of better conditions for humanity, of higher ideals; his dream of a larger, finer type of manhood ; of better government, of a finer citizenship, of a larger and cleaner manhood and womanhood.

The child lives in dreamland. It creates a world of its own, and plays with the castles it builds. It traces pictures which are very real to it; it enjoys that which was never on sea or land, but which has a powerful influence in shaping its future life and character.

Do not stop dreaming. Encourage your visions and believe in them. Cherish your dreams and try to make them real. This thing in us that aspires, that bids us to look tup, that beckons us higher, is God-given. Aspiration is the hand that points us to the road that runs heavenward. As your vision is, so will your life be. Your better dream is the prophecy of what your life may be, ought to be.

The great thing is to try to fashion the life after the pattern shown us in the moment of our highest inspiration; *to make our highest moment permanent.*

We are all conscious that the best we do is but a sorry apology for what we ought to do, might do. The average man is but a burlesque of the sublime man God intended him to be. We certainly were made for something larger, grander, and more beautiful than we are. We have a feeling that what we are is out of keeping with does not fit the larger, greater life-plan which the Creator patterned for us; that it is mean, sordid, stingy, and pinched compared with the pattern of that divine man shown us in the moment of our highest vision.

It is this creative power of the imagination, these dreams of the dreamers made good, that will ultimately raise man to his highest power ; that will break down the barriers of caste, race, and creed, and make real the poet's vision of the Parliament of man, the Federation of the world.

" *The Golden 'Age lies onward, not behind.*
The pathway through the past has led us up:
The pathway through the future will lead on, And higher. "

VI.

THE SPIRIT IN WHICH YOU WORK

IT ought not to be necessary to ask a man if he likes his work. The radiance of his face should tell that. His very buoyancy and pride in his task; his spirit of unbounded enthusiasm and zest, ought to show. it. He ought to be so in love with his work that he finds his greatest delight in it ; and this inward joy should light up his whole being.

A test of the quality of the individual is the spirit in which he does his work. If he goes to it grudgingly, like a slave under the lash; if he feels the drudgery in it ; if his enthusiasm and love for it do not lift it out of commonness and make it a delight instead of a bore, he will never make a very great place for himself in the world.

The man who feels his life-yoke galling him ; who does not understand why the 'bread-and-butter question could not have been solved by one great creative act, instead of every man's being obliged to wrench everything he gets from nature through hard work ; the man who does not see a beneficent design and a superb necessity in the principle that every one should earn his own living has gotten a wrong view of life, and will never get the splendid results out of his vocation that were intended for him.

Multitudes of people do not half respect their work. They look upon it as a disagreeable necessity for providing bread and butter, clothing and shelter as unavoidable drudgery, instead of as a great man builder, a great life university for the development of manhood and womanhood. They do not see the divinity in the spur of necessity which compels man to develop the best thing in him; to unfold his possibilities by his struggle to attain his ambition, to conquer the enemies of his prosperity and his happiness. They cannot see the curse in the unearned dollar, which takes the spur out of the motive. Work to them is sheer drudgery an unmitigated evil. They cannot understand why the Creator did not put bread ready-made on trees. They do not see the stamina, the grit, the nobility, and the manhood in being forced to conquer what they get. No one can make a real success of his life when he is all the time grumbling or apologizing for what he is doing. It is a confession of weakness.

What a pitiable sight to see one of God's noblemen, made to hold up his head and be a king, to be cheerful and happy and to radiate power, going about whining and complaining of his work, even deploring the fact that he should have to work at all ! It is demoralizing to allow yourself to do a thing in a half-hearted, grudging manner.

There is a great adaptive power in human nature. The mind is wonderfully adjustive to different conditions; but you will not get the best results until your mind is settled, until you are resolved not only to like your work, but also to do it in the spirit of a master and not in that of a slave. Resolve that, whatever you do, you will bring the whole man to it; that you will fling the whole weight of your being into it; that you will do it in the spirit of a conqueror, and so get the lesson and power out of it which come only to the conqueror.

Put the right spirit into your work. Treat your calling as divine *as a call from principle.* If the thing itself be not important, the spirit in which you take hold of it makes all the difference in the world to you. It can make or mar the man. You cannot afford grumbling service or botched work in your life's record. You cannot afford to form a habit of half doing things, or of doing them in the spirit of a drudge, for this will drag its slimy trail through all your subsequent career, always humiliating you at the most unexpected times. Let other people do the poor jobs, the botched work, if they will. Keep your standards up, your ideals high.

The attitude with which a man approaches his task has everything to do with the quality and efficiency of his work, and with its influence upon his character. What a man does is a part of himself. It is the expression of what he stands for. Our life-work is an outpicturing of our ambition, our ideals, our real selves. If you see a man's work you see the man.

No one can respect himself, or have that sublime faith in himself, which is essential to all high achievement, when he puts mean, half-hearted, slipshod service into what he does. He cannot get his highest self approval until he does his level best. No man can do his best, or call out the highest thing in him, while he regards his occupation as drudgery or a bore.

Under no circumstances allow yourself to do anything as a drudge. Nothing is more demoralizing. No matter if circumstances force you to do something which is distasteful, compel yourself to find something interesting and instructive in it. Everything that is necessary to be done is full of interest. It is all a question of the attitude of mind in which we go to our task.

If your occupation is distasteful, every rebellious thought, every feeling of disgust, only surrounds you with a failure atmosphere which is sure to attract more failure. The magnet that brings success and happiness must be charged with a positive, optimistic, enthusiastic force.

The man who has not learned the secret of taking the drudgery out of his task by flinging his whole soul into it, has not learned the first principles of success or happiness. It is perfectly possible to so exalt the most ordinary business, by bringing to it the spirit of a master, as to make of it a dignified vocation.

The trouble with us is that we drop into a humdrum existence and do our work mechanically, with no heart, no vim, and no purpose. We do not learn the fine art of living for growth, for mind and soul expansion. We just exist.

It was not intended that any necessary employment should be merely commonplace. There is a great, deep meaning in it all a glory in it. Our possibilities, our destiny are in it, and the good of the world.

Why is it that most people think that the glory of life does not belong to the ordinary vocations that this belongs to the artist, to the musician, to the writer, or to some one of the more gentle and what they call "dignified " professions ? There is as much dignity and grandeur and glory in agriculture as in statesmanship or authorship.

Some people never see any beauty anywhere. They have no soul for the beautiful. Others see it everywhere. Farming to one man is a humdrum existence, an unbearable vocation, a monotonous routine; while another sees the glory and the dignity in it, and takes infinite pleasure in mixing brains with the soil and in working with the Creator to produce grander results.

I knew a cobbler in a little village who took infinitely more pride in his vocation than did the lawyer, or even the clergyman, of that town. I know a farmer who takes more pride in his crops than any other person in his community takes in his calling. He walks over his farm as proudly as a monarch might travel through his kingdom. This true master-farmer will introduce his visitor to his horses and cows and other animals as though they were important personages. That is the kind of enthusiasm that takes the drudgery out of the farm and makes a joy out of a life which to many is so dull and commonplace.

I have known a stenographer on small pay who put a higher quality of effort into her work than the proprietor of the great establishment she worked for, and she got more out of life than he did. I knew a school-teacher in a little district twenty-five miles from a rail-road, in a schoolhouse right in the forest, who look more pride in her work and in the progress of her pupils than some presidents of colleges whom I have known appeared to take in their duties.

A girl who declared that she never would do housework; that she never would cook, no matter what misfortunes might come to her; married a man who lost his money, and she was forced to part with her servants and to do the cooking herself for the family. She thought she never could do it, but she determined to make bread making an art; to elevate cooking and make it a science in her home; and she succeeded.

No matter how humble your work may seem, do it in the spirit of an artist, of a master. In this way you lift it out of commonness and rob it of what would otherwise be drudgery.

You will find that learning to thoroughly respect everything you do, and not to let it go out of your hands until it has the stamp of your approval upon it as a trademark, will have a wonderful effect upon your whole character.

The quality of your work will have a great deal to do with the quality of your life. If your work quality is down, your character will be down, your standards down, your ideals down. The habit of insisting upon the best of which you are capable, and of always demanding of yourself the highest, never accepting the lowest, will make all the difference between mediocrity or failure, and a successful career.

If you bring to your work the spirit of an artist, instead of an artisan if you bring a burning zeal, an all-absorbing enthusiasm if you determine to put the best there is in you in everything you do, no matter what it is, you will not long be troubled with a sense of drudgery. Everything depends on the spirit we bring the task. The right spirit makes an artist in the humblest task, while the wrong spirit makes an artisan in any calling, no matter how high that calling may be.

There is a dignity, an indescribable quality of superiority, in everything we do which we thoroughly and honestly respect. There is nothing belittling or menial which has to be done for the welfare of the race. You cannot afford to give the mere dregs, the mere leavings of your energies, to your work. The best in you is none too good for it.

It is only when we do our best, when we put joy, energy, enthusiasm and zeal into our work, that we really grow ; and this is the only way we can keep our highest self-respect.

We cannot think much of ourselves when we are not honest in our work when we are not doing our level best. There is nothing which will compensate you for the loss of faith in yourself; for the knowledge of your reputation for doing bungling, dishonest work.

You have something infinitely higher within you to satisfy than to make a mere living, to get through your day's work as easily as possible. It is your sense of right; the demand within you to do your level best; to develop the highest thing in you; to do the square thing to be a man. This should speak so loudly in you that the mere bread-and-butter question, the money-making question, should be absolutely insignificant in comparison.

Start out with the tacit understanding with yourself that you will be a man at all hazards; that your work shall express the highest and the best things in you, and that you cannot afford to debase or demoralize yourself, by appealing to the lowest, the most despicable, mean side of yourself by deteriorating, by botching your work.

How often we see people working along without purpose, half committed to their aim, only intending to pursue their vocation until they strike snags! They intend to keep at it as long as it is tolerable, or until they find something they like better. This is a cowardly way to face a life-work which determines our destiny.

A man ought to approach his life task, however humble, with the high ideals that characterize a great master as he approaches the canvas upon which he is going to put his masterpiece with a resolution to make no false moves that will mar the model that lives in his ideal.

A sacred thing, this, approaching the uncut marble of life. We cannot afford to strike any false blows which might mar the angel that sleeps in the stone; for the image we produce must represent our life-work. Whether it is beautiful or hideous, divine or brutal, it must stand as an expression of ourselves, as representing our ideals.

It always pains me to see a young person approaching his life-work with carelessness and indifference, as though it did not make much difference to him how he did his work if he only got through with it and got his pay for it. How little the average youth realizes the sacredness, the dignity, the divinity of his calling !

There is a higher meaning, something broader, deeper, and nobler in a vocation than making a living or seeking fame. Making a life is the best thing in it. It should be a man developer, a character-builder, and a great life school for broadening, deepening, and rounding into symmetry, harmony, and beauty all the God-given faculties within us.

The part of our life-work which gives us a living, which provides the bread and butter and clothes and houses and shelter, is merely incidental to the great disciplinary, educative phase of it the self-unfoldment. It is a question of how large and how grand a man or woman you can bring out of your vocation, not how much money there is in it.

Your life-work is your statue. You cannot get away from it. It is beautiful or hideous, lovely or ugly, inspiring or debasing, as you make it. It will elevate or degrade. You can no more get away from it than you can, of your own volition, rise from the earth.

Every errand you do, every letter you write, every piece of merchandise you sell, every conversation, every thought of yours everything you do or think is a blow of the chisel which mars or beautifies the statue.

The attitude of mind with which we perform our life-work colors the whole career and determines the quality of the destiny. It is the lofty ideal that redeems the life from the curse of commonness, and imparts a touch of nobility to every calling. But a low, sordid aim will take the dignity out of any occupation.

VII.

RESPONSIBILITY DEVELOPS POWER

THERE is enough latent force in a Maximite torpedo shell to tear a warship to pieces. But the amount of force or explosive power in one of these terrific engines of destruction could never be ascertained by any ordinary concussion.

Children could play with it for years, pound it, roll it about, and do all sorts of things with it; the shell might be shot through the walls of an ordinary building, without arousing its terrible dynamic energy. It must be fired from a cannon, with terrific force, through a foot or so of steel plate armor, before it meets with resistance great enough to evoke its mighty explosive power.

Every man is a stranger to his greatest strength, his mightiest power, until the test of a great responsibility, a critical emergency, or a supreme crisis in his life, calls it out.

Work on a farm, hauling wood, working in a tannery, storekeeping, West Point, the Mexican War, doing odd jobs about town, were not enough to arouse the sleeping giant in General Grant. There is no probability that he would ever have been heard from outside of his own little community but for the emergency of the Civil War.

There was a tremendous dynamic force in the man, but it required the concussion of the great Civil War to ignite it. No ordinary occasion touched his slumbering power, no ordinary experience could ignite the powder in this giant. Under common circumstances he would have gone through life a stranger to his own ability, just as most of the great dynamite shells now in existence will probably never be exploded because of the lack of a war emergency great enough to explode them.

Farming, wood-chopping, rail-splitting, surveying, storekeeping, the state legislature, the practice of law, not even the United States Congress, furnished occasions great enough, resistance strong enough, to ignite the spark of power, to explode the dynamic force in Abraham Lincoln. Only the responsibility of a nation in imminent peril furnished sufficient concussion to ignite the giant powder in perhaps the greatest man that ever trod the American Continent.

There is no probability that Lincoln would have gone down in history as a very great man but for the crisis of the Civil War. The nation's peril was the responsibility thrust up on him which brought out the last ounce of his reserves, his latent power of achievement, the resources which never would have dreamed he possessed but for this emergency.

Some of the greatest men in history never discovered themselves until they lost everything but their pluck and grit, or until some great misfortune overtook them and they were driven to desperation to invent a way out of their dilemma.

Giants are made in the stern school of necessity. The strong, vigorous, forceful, stalwart men who have pushed civilization upward are the products of self-help. They have not been pushed or boosted; but they have fought every inch of the way up to their own loaf.

They are giants because they have been great conquerors of difficulties, supreme masters of difficult situations. They have acquired the strength of the obstacles which they have overcome.

Many of our giant business men never got a glimpse of their real power until some great panic or misfortune swept their property away and knocked the crutches out from under them. Many men and women never discovered their ability until everything they thought would help them to success had been taken away from them; until they had been stripped of everything that they held dear in life. Our greatest power, our highest possibility, lies so deep in our natures that it often takes a tremendous emergency, a powerful crisis, to call it out. It is only when we feel that all bridges behind us are burned, all retreat cut off, and that we have no outside aid to lean upon, that we discover our full inherent power. As long as we get outside help we never know our own resources. How many young men and young women owe their success to some great misfortune, which cut off a competence the death of a relative, the loss of business or home, or some other great calamity, which threw them on their own resources and compelled them to fight for themselves!

Responsibility is a great power developer. Where there is responsibility there is growth. People who are never thrust into responsible positions never develop their real strength. This is one reason why it is so rare to find very strong men and women among those who have spent their lives in subordinate positions, in the service of others. They go through life comparative weaklings because their powers have never been tested or developed by having great responsibility thrust up on them. Their thinking has been done for them. They have simply carried out somebody else's programme. They have never learned to stand alone, to think for themselves, to act independently. Because they have never been obliged to plan for themselves, they have never developed the best things in them, their power of originality, inventiveness, initiative, independence, self-reliance, their possible grit and stamina. The power to create, to make combinations, to meet emergencies, the power which comes from continuous marshaling of one's forces to meet difficult situations, to adjust means to ends, that stamina or power which makes one equal to the great crisis in the life of a nation, is only developed by years of practical training under great responsibility.

There is nothing more misleading than the philosophy that if there is anything in a youth it will come out. It may come out, and it may not. It depends largely upon circumstances, upon the presence or absence of an ambition-arousing, a grit-awakening environment. The greatest ability is not always accompanied by the greatest confidence or the greatest ambition.

There is at this moment enough power latent in the clerks or ordinary employees in almost any of our business houses to manage them as well as, or better than they are being managed today, if the opportunity and necessary emergency to call out this dynamic force should arise.

But how can clerks who remain behind counters, measuring cloth, selling shoes or hosiery, year in and year out, ever know what latent power for organization, what executive ability or initiative they possess?

It is true that some of the more ambitious and courageous get out and start for themselves, but it does not follow that they are always abler than those who remain behind. Sometimes the greatest ability is accompanied by great modesty and even timidity. Then, again, employees conscious of great ability are often deterred from taking the risk of launching out for themselves because of possible disaster to those depending upon them for daily bread. But thrust great responsibility upon a man, drive him to desperation, and the demand will bring out what there is in him. It will call out his initiative, his ingenuity, his resourcefulness, his self-reliance, his power to adjust means to ends. If there are any elements of leadership in him, responsibility will call them out. It will test his power to do things.

I have in mind a young man who developed such amazing ability within six months from the date of a very important promotion, that he surprised everybody who knew him. Even his best friends did not believe that it was in him. But the great responsibilities, the desperate situation, thrust upon him brought out his reserve power, and he very quickly showed of what stuff he was made. This promotion, and a little stock in the concern, which had been given him, aroused his ambition and called out a mighty power which before he did not dream that he possessed.

Tens of thousands of young men and young women to-day are only waiting for a chance to show themselves, waiting for an opportunity to try their wings, and when the opportunity, the responsibility, comes they will be equal to anything that confronts them.

Proprietors of large concerns are often very much exercised by the death of a superintendent or lieutenant who has managed with exceptional ability. They are fearful that very disastrous results may follow, and believe it will be almost impossible to fill his place; but, while they are looking around to find a man big enough for the place, some one, perhaps, who was under the former chief, attends to his duties temporarily, and makes even a better manager than his predecessor.

Young men and young women are rising out of the ranks constantly, everywhere, who fill these positions often times much better than those who drop out and whose places it was thought almost impossible to fill. Do not be afraid to pile responsibility upon your employees, You will be amazed to see how quickly they will get out from under their load and what unexpected ability they will develop.

Many employers are always looking for people outside of their own establishment to fill important vacancies, simply because they cannot see or appreciate a man's ability until he has actually demonstrated it; but how can he demonstrate it until he has the chance?

There are probably today scores of young men in every one of our great business houses who are as capable as the present heads. There is no position that cannot be filled as well or better than it is being filled now, by someone who is still in the ranks and who has not yet been heard from in any distinctive way.

When some great statesman falls, the people often look about, to find that there is apparently no one to fill his place; but from an unexpected source perhaps from a little out-of-the-way town, from the common ranks there comes a man who is equal to the emergency.

The way to bring out the reserve in a man is to pile responsibility upon him. If there is anything in him this will reveal it.

Some of us never quite come to ourselves in fullness and power until driven to desperation. It is when we are shipwrecked like Robinson Crusoe upon an island, with nothing but our own brain and hands, nothing but resources locked up deep in ourselves, that we really come to complete self-discovery. A captain never knows what is in his men until they have been tested by a gale at sea which threatens shipwreck.

That there are great potencies and power possibilities within us which we may never know is proved by the tremendous forces that are aroused in ordinary people in some great crisis or emergency.

The elevator boy may never have dreamed that there was anything heroic in his nature. He may never have thought there was a possibility of his rising in the world to the importance of the men whom he lifted to their offices ; but the building takes fire and this boy, who was seldom noticed by anyone, who did not show any special signs of ability, in a few minutes develops the most heroic qualities. He runs his elevator up through the burning floors when choked with smoke, the hot cable blistering his hands, and rescues a hundred people who, but for him, might have lost their lives.

A ship is wrecked at sea, and a poor immigrant becomes the hero of the hour, commanding a lifeboat, and giving orders with calmness, authority, and force, when others have lost their heads.

A hospital takes fire and the delicate, timid girl invalid develops into a heroine almost instantly and does a giant's work.

In fires and wrecks, in great disasters or emergencies of all kinds, are enacted deeds of daring and of sublime heroism which, before the great test came, would have been thought impossible by those who did them.

No one ever knows just how much dynamic force there is in him until tested by a great emergency or a supreme crisis. Oftentimes men reach middle life, and even later, before they really discover themselves. Until some great emergency, loss, or sorrow, has tested their timber they cannot tell how much strain they can stand. No emergency great enough to call out their latent power ever before confronted them, and they did not themselves realize what they would be equal to until the great crisis confronted them.

I have known of several instances where daughters reared in luxury were suddenly thrown upon their own resources by the death of their parents and the loss of their inherited fortunes. They had not been brought up to work, did not know how to do anything useful, had no trade, and no idea how to earn a livelihood; and yet all at once they developed marvelous ability for doing things. The power was there, latent ; but responsibility had not hitherto been thrust upon them.

Young men suddenly forced into positions of tremendous responsibility by accident or death are often not the same men in six months. They have developed strong manly qualities which no one ever dreamed they possessed. Responsibility has made men of them. And it makes women of inexperienced and untried girls who are suddenly thrust into an emergency where they are obliged to conduct a business or support a family.

Many people distrust their initiative because they have not had an opportunity to exercise it. The monotonous routine of doing the same work year in and year out does not tend to develop new faculties. All the mental powers must be exercised, strengthened, before we can measure their possibilities.

I know young men who believe in everybody but themselves. They seem to have no doubt about other people accomplishing what they undertake, but are always shaky about themselves: " Oh, do not put me at the head of this or that ; somebody else can do it better than I." They shrink from responsibility because they lack self-faith.

The only way to develop power is to resolve early in life never to let an opportunity for doing so go by.

Never shrink from anything which will give you more discipline, better training, and enlarged experience. No matter how distasteful force yourself into it. There is nothing like responsibility for developing ability. Never mind if the position is hard ; take it and make up your mind that you are going to fill it better than it was ever before filled.

I once heard a man say he regretted more than anything else in his life that he had indulged his natural inclination to decline every position of responsibility offered him. He was naturally so shy that any position which attracted attention or gave him the least publicity was distasteful to him. His magnificent possibilities remain undeveloped because he has never had that responsibility which calls out one's reserves and develops his latent powers. Many a time he thought he would change his course, and made up his mind never to let another opportunity for self-development go by him unimproved. But the habit of delaying until he should be better prepared got such a hold of him that he could not change. The result is that, although he is a man of recognized power, with a superb mind, his life has been an extremely quiet one, very tame and unimportant compared with what it would have been had he made it a rule to thrust himself into every position of responsibility which would have called out the best in him.

Many people never discover themselves or know their possibilities because they always shrink from responsibility. They lease themselves to somebody else and die with their greatest possibilities unreleased, undeveloped.

Personally, I believe it is the duty of every young person to have an ambition to be independent, to be his own master, and to resolve that he will not be at somebody else's call all his life come and go at the sounding of a gong or the touch of a bell that he will at least belong to himself; that he will be an entire wheel and not a cog; that he will be a whole machine, although it may be a small one, rather than part of someone else's machine.

The very stretching of the mind toward high ideals, the looking forward to the time when we shall be our own masters, working along the lines of a resolution, a fixed, irrevocable determination, has a strengthening, unifying influence upon all of the faculties, and you will be a stronger man or woman, whatever your future, if you keep steadily, persistently in mind your own individual declaration of independence. It means freedom, it means delivery from restraint, from a certain feeling of slavery which attaches to every subordinate position. I do not believe that it is possible for any one to reach the same magnitude of manhood or womanhood, to grow to the same statute, after giving up the struggle for absolute independence or the hope of going into a business or profession or something else *all of one's own.*

It is true that not every person has the executive ability or strength of mind, the qualities of leadership, the moral stamina, or the push to conduct a business successfully for himself and stand his ground. There are, also, many instances of young men who have others dependent upon them, and who are not in a position to take the risks of going into business for themselves. A great many, however, work for others merely because they do not dare to take the risk of starting on their own responsibility. They lack the courage to branch out. The fear of possible failure deters them. Moreover, a great many start as boys in certain occupations, work up to a fairly good salary, and, though they may be ambitious to be independent, are yet held back by the distrust of their own powers and the advice of others, to " let well enough alone," until the habit of doing the same thing year in and year out becomes so fixed that it is very difficult to wrench themselves out of their environment.

Again, a great many people prefer a small certainty to a big uncertainty. There is no disposition to hazard, no desire to take risks, in their make-up. They do not want to assume large responsibilities. They prefer steady employment, and the certainty that every Saturday night they will find fixed sums in their pay envelopes, to the great risks, responsibilities, and uncertainties of a business of their own.

You may not have the ambition, the desire, or the inclination to take responsibility. You may prefer to have an easier life, and to let somebody else worry about the payment of notes and debts, the hard times, the dull seasons, and the panics. But, if you expect to bring out the greatest possibilities in you, if growth, with the largest possible expansion of your powers, is your goal, you cannot realize your ambition in the ***fullest and completest*** sense while merely trying to carry out somebody else's programme and letting him furnish the ideas.

There must be a sense of complete independence, not partial but complete, in order to reach the highest growth. We do not attain our full stature of manhood or womanhood in captivity or in slavery, but in freedom, in absolute liberty. The eagle must be let out of the cage, no matter how large or how comfortable, before it can exhibit all the powers of an eagle.

It is the locked-up forces within, that lie deep in our natures, not those which are on the surface, that test our mettle. It is within everybody's power to call out these hidden forces, to be somebody and to do something worth while in the world, and the man who does not do it is violating his sacred birthright.

Every man or woman who goes through the world with great continents of undiscovered possibilities locked up within him commits a sin against himself and that which borders on a crime against civilization.

Don't be afraid to trust yourself. Have faith in your own ability to think along original lines. If there is anything in you, self-reliance will bring it out.

Whatever you do, cultivate a spirit of manly independence in doing it. ***Let your work express yourself.*** Don't be a mere cog in a machine. Do your own thinking and carry out your own ideas, as far as possible, even though working for another.

VIII.

AN OVERMASTERING PURPOSE

BEFORE water generates steam, it must register two hundred and twelve degrees of heat. Two hundred degrees will not do it; two hundred and ten will not do it. The water must boil before it will generate enough steam to move an engine, to run a train. Lukewarm water will not run anything.

A great many people are trying to move their life trains with luke warm water or water that is almost boiling and they are wondering why they are stalled, why they can not get ahead. They are trying to run a boiler with two hundred or two hundred and ten degrees of heat, and they cannot understand why they do not get anywhere.

Lukewarmness in his work stands in the same relation to man's achievement as lukewarm water does to the locomotive boiler. No man can hope to accomplish anything great in this world until he throws his whole soul, flings the force of his whole life, into it.

In Phillips Brooks's talks to young people he used to urge them to *be something with all their might.* It is not enough simply to have a general desire to be something. There is but one way to accomplish it; and that is, to strive to be somebody with all the concentrated energy we can muster. Any kind of a human being can wish for a thing, can desire it; but only strong, vigorous minds with great purposes can do things.

There is an infinite distance between the wishers and the doers. A mere desire is lukewarm water, which never will take a train to its destination; the purpose must boil, must be made into live steam to do the work.

Who would ever have heard of Theodore Roosevelt outside of his immediate community if he had only half committed himself to what he had undertaken; if he had brought only a part of himself to his task? The great secret of his career has been that he has flung his whole life, not a part of it, with all the determination and energy and power he could muster, into everything he has undertaken. No dillydallying, no faint-hearted efforts, no lukewarm purpose for him!

Every life of power must have a great master purpose which takes precedence of all other motives a supreme principle which is so commanding and so imperative in its demands for recognition and exercise that there can be no mistaking its call. Without this the water of energy will never reach the boiling point; the life train will not get anywhere.

The man with a vigorous purpose is a positive, constructive, creative force. No one can be resourceful, inventive, original, or creative without powerful concentration; and the undivided focusing of the mind is only possible along the line of the ambition, the life purpose. We cannot focus the mind upon a thing we are not interested in and enthusiastic about.

A man ought to look upon his career as a great artist looks upon his masterpiece, as an outpicturing of his best self, upon which he dwells with infinite pride and a satisfaction which nothing else can give. Yet many people are so loosely connected with their vocation that they are easily separated from it.

I know young men who seem anxious to get on in their careers, but in a single evening they could be induced to give up their calling for something else. They are always wondering whether they are in the right place, or where their ability will count most. They lose heart when they strike obstacles; or they become discouraged when they hear of some one else who has made a success in some other line, and wonder if they had not better try something in the same line. If one is so loosely attached to his occupation that he can be easily induced to give it up, you may be sure that he is not in the right place. If nature has called you to a position, if the call runs in your blood, it is a part of your life and you cannot get away from it. It is not a separate thing from yourself. It exists in every brain cell, every nerve cell; every blood corpuscle contains some of it. You can no more get away from it than a leopard can get away from his spots. So when a young man asks me if I do not think he had better make a change, I feel very certain that he is not in the place God called him to, for the thing he was made for is as much a part of his real being as his temperament. It is nearer to him than his heart-beat, closer than his breath. There is a photograph of the thing he was made for, in every cell in his body. He cannot get away from it.

The thing which will make the life distinctive, which will make it a power, is the one supreme thing which we want to do, and feel that we must do; and, no matter how long we may be delayed from this aim, or how far we may be swerved aside by mistakes or iron circumstances, we should never give up hope or a determination to pursue our object.

Some people have not the moral courage, the persistence, the force of character, to get the things out of the way which stand between them and their ambition. They allow themselves to be pushed this way and that way into things for which they have no fitness or taste. Their will power is not strong enough to enable them to fight their way to their goal. They are pushed aside by the pressure about them, and do the things for which they have little or no liking or adaptation.

If there is anything in the world a person should fight for, it is freedom to pursue his ideal, because in that is his great opportunity for self-expression, for the unfoldment of the greatest thing possible to him. It is his great chance to make his life tell in the largest, completest way; to do the most original, distinctive thing possible to him.

If he does not pursue his ideal, does not carry out his supreme aim, his life will be more or less of a failure, no matter how much he may be actuated by a sense of duty, or how much he may exert his will power to over-come his handicap.

There is great power in a resolution that has no reservation in it a strong, persistent, tenacious purpose which burns all bridges behind it, clears all obstacles from its path, and arrives at its goal, no matter how long it may take, no matter what the sacrifice or the cost.

The inspiration of a great, positive aim transforms the life and revolutionizes a shiftless, ambitionless, dissipated, good-for-nothing man as if some divine energy had worked in him even as love sometimes transforms an **slovenly**, purposeless, coarse man into a clean, methodical, diviner being.

When the awakening power of a new purpose, a resolute aim, is born in a man, he is a new creature. He sees everything in a new light. The doubts, the fears, the apathy, the vicious temptations which dogged his steps but yesterday, the stagnation which had blighted his past life, all vanish as if by magic. They are dispelled by the breath of a new purpose. Beauty and system take the place of unsightliness and confusion. Order reigns in the place of anarchy. All his slumbering faculties awaken to activity. The effect of this new ambition is like the clarifying change made by a water-way in a stagnant, swampy district. The water clarifies as soon as it begins to move, to do something ; flowers spring up in place of poisonous weeds; and vegetation, beauty, birds and song make joyous the once miasmic atmosphere.

Chemists tell us that when a compound is broken up and an atom is released from the attraction of other atoms, it takes on new energy and immediately seeks combination with another free atom; but the longer it remains alone, the weaker it becomes. It seems to lose much of its vitality and power of attraction when idle.

When the atom is first freed from the grasp of its fellows, it is called nascent " new born." It is then that it has its maximum of gripping power; and if it finds a free atom immediately after it is released, it will unite with it with greater vigor than ever. The power seems to go out of it, if it delays its union with another atom.

Mythology tells us that Minerva, the goddess of Wisdom, sprang complete, full-orbed, full-grown, from Jupiter's brain. Man's highest conception, his most effective thought, most inventive and resourceful ideas, and grandest visions spring full-orbed, complete, with their maximum of power, spontaneously from the brain. Men who postpone their visions, who delay the execution of their ideas, who bottle up their thoughts, to be used at a more convenient time, are always weaklings. The forceful, vigorous, effective men are those who execute their ideas while they are full of the enthusiasm of inspiration.

Our ideas, our visions, our resolutions come to us fresh every day, because this is the divine programme for the day, not for tomorrow.

Another inspiration, new ideas will come to-morrow. To-day we should carry out the inspiration of the day.

A divine vision flashes across the artist's mind with lightning-like rapidity, but it is not convenient for him to seize his brush and fasten the immortal vision before it fades. He keeps turning it over and over in his mind. It takes possession of his very soul, but he is not in his studio, or it is not convenient to put his divine vision upon canvas, and the picture gradually fades from his mind.

A strong, vigorous conception flashes into the brain of the writer, and he has an almost irresistible impulse to seize his pen and transfer the beautiful images and the fascinating conception to paper; but it is not convenient at the moment, and, while it seems almost impossible to wait, he postpones the writing. The images and the conception keep haunting him, but he still postpones. Finally the visions grow dimmer and dimmer, and at hast fade away and are lost forever.

There is a reason for all this. Why do we have these strong, vigorous impulses; these divine visions of splendid possibilities? Why do they come to us with such rapidity and vigor, such vividness and suddenness?

It is because it is intended that we shall use them while fresh, execute them while the inclination is hot. Our ideas, our visions are like the manna of the wilderness, which the Israelites were obliged to gather fresh every day. If they undertook to hoard it, it became stale, the nourishment evaporated, the life went out of it. They could not use old manna.

There is something about allowing a strong resolution to evaporate without executing it that has a deteriorating influence upon the character. It is the execution of a plan that makes stamina. Almost anybody can resolve to do a great thing; it is only the strong, determined character that puts the resolve into execution.

If we could only make our highest moments permanent, what splendid things we should do in life, and what magnificent beings we should become; but we let our resolutions cool, our visions fade until it is more convenient to execute them, and they are gone.

There is no easier way in which one can hypnotize or deceive himself than by thinking that because he is always making great resolutions he is doing something worth while or carrying them out.

I know a man who would feel insulted if any one were to intimate that he had not been a hard worker, and had not accomplished a great deal in life; and yet, although he is an able man, his whole life has been spent in jumping out of one thing and into another so quickly that one could scarcely see the change. Yet every time you see him he carries his head high, he is as enthusiastic and optimistic as though his whole life had been one triumphant march. His enthusiasm is intense but it fades away just as quickly as it came. The very fact that he always lives in the clouds, is always dreaming of the great things he is going to do, seems to convince him that he actually does them. But he never stays at one thing long enough to reach effectiveness. His whole life has been spent in *starting things brilliantly* and enthusiastically; few men have ever begun so many things as he, or completed so few.

The putting-off habit will kill the strongest initiative. Too much caution and lack of confidence are fatal enemies of initiative. How much easier it is to do a thing when the purpose impels us, when enthusiasm carries us along, than when everything drags in the postponement! One is drudgery, the other delight.

Hungering and striving after knowledge is what makes a scholar; hungering and striving after virtue is what makes a saint; hungering and striving after noble action is what makes a hero and a man. The great successes we see everywhere are but the realization of an intense longing, a concentrated effort. Everyone is gravitating toward his aim just in proportion to the power and intensity of his desire, and his struggle to realize it.

One merely " desires " to do this or that, or " wishes " he could, or " would be glad " if he could. Another knows perfectly well that, if he lives, he is going to do the thing he sets his heart on if it is within the limits of human possibility. We do not hear him whining because nobody will pay his way to college. He does not say he "wishes" he could go. He says, " I am going to prepare myself for a great life-work. I have faith in my future. I have made a vow to myself to succeed, and I am going to do so on a broad-gauge plan. I am not going to start out half equipped, half fitted. I will have a college training."

When you find a boy who resolves within himself that, come what will, he is going to do the thing he sets his heart on, and that there are no" " Ifs" " or " buts " or " ands " about it, you may be sure he is made of winning stuff. He will not postpone and postpone the realization of his vision until too late, until its glory has vanished. He will lose no time in putting forth all his energy to make it real, and, if it is a possible thing he will succeed.

IX.

HAS YOUR VOCATION YOUR UNQUALIFIED APPROVAL?

QUOTE the following sentences from a letter just received. " In your February editorial, the following paragraph has impressed me mightily: ' To spend a life in buying and selling lies, or cheap, shoddy shams, is demoralizing to every element of nobility, to excellence in any form.' Now, I happen to be in the sham business and hate it so heartily that I want to get out of it as soon as I can do so with justice to others' interests."

This young man, who gets more than ten thousand dollars a year in salary, says that he is expected to " trade upon the credulity of the poorer classes, who can ill afford to be preyed upon," and he continues:

"While I need the money, I cannot enjoy this kind of work, nor can I write with conviction or ambition on projects which I naturally know to be fakes. Besides, I am afraid of the very thing pointed out in your editorial ; namely, growing down to the work. I hate hypocrisy worse than any other thing, and I cannot do my best work in any business based on such a foundation. I do not want to remain in an occupation which pays its highest salaries to the most skillful fakirs."

It is pitiable to see a strong, bright, promising young man, capable of filling a high position, trying to support himself and his family in an occupation which has not received his approval, which is lowering his ideals, which dwarfs his nature, which makes him despise himself, which strangles all that is best and noblest within him, and which is constantly condemning him and ostracizing him and his family from all that is best and truest in life.

How often we hear a young man say: "I do not like the business I am in. I know it has a bad influence on me. I do not believe in the methods used, or the deceptions practiced. I am ashamed to have my friends know what I am doing, and I say as little about it in public as possible. I know I ought to change, but it is the only business I understand in which I can earn as much money as I need to keep up appearances, for I have been getting a good salary and have contracted expensive habits of living, and I have not the "force of character to risk a change."

Do not deceive yourself with the idea that somebody has got to do this questionable work, and that it might as well be you. Let other people do it, if they will; there is something better for you. The Creator has given you a guarantee, written in your blood and brain cells, that if you keep yourself clean and do that which he has indicated in your very constitution, you will be a man, will succeed, and will belong to the order of true nobility; but if you do not heed that edict, you will fail. You may get a large salary, but this alone is not success. If the almighty dollar is dragging its slimy trail all through your career; if money-making has become your one unwavering aim, you have failed, no matter how much you have accumulated. If your money smells of the blood of the innocent, if there is a dirty dollar in it, if there is a taint of avarice in it, if envy and greed have helped in its accumulation, if there is a sacrifice of the rights and comforts of others in it, if there is a stain of dishonor on your stocks and bonds, or if a smirched character looms up in your pile, do not boast of your success, for you have failed. Making money by dirty work is bad business, gild it how we will.

There are a thousand indications in you that the Creator did not fit you for what is wrong, but only for the right. Do the right, and all nature, all law, and all science will help you, because the attainment of rectitude is the plan of the universe. It is the very nature of things. Reverse it, and all these forces are pledged to defeat you.

To the young men who have written for advice, let me say that if you are making money by forcing yourself by sheer will power to do what you loathe, what does not engage your whole heart, or that into which you cannot fling your entire being, because you fear that it is not quite right, you can do a thousand times better in an occupation which has your unreserved, unqualified consent. If you refuse to smirch your ability, no matter what the reward, you will thereby increase your success-power a thousandfold.

The very fact that you can come out of a questionable situation boldly and take a stand for the right, regardless of consequences, will help you immeasurably. The greater self-respect, increased self-confidence, and the tonic influence which will come from the sense of victory, will give you the air of a conqueror instead of that of one conquered. Nobody ever loses anything by standing for the right with decision, with firmness, and with vigor.

You have a compass within you, the needle of which points more surely to the right and to the true than the needle of the mariner points to the pole star. If you do not follow it you are in perpetual danger of going to pieces on the rocks. Your conscience is your compass, given you when you were launched upon life's high seas. It is the only guide that is sure to take you safely into the harbor of true success.

What if a mariner should refuse to steer by the pointing of his compass, declaring it to be all nonsense that the needle should always point north, and should pull it around so that it would point in some other direction, fasten it there, and then sail by it ? He would never reach port in safety.

It takes only a little influence just a little force, to pull the needle away from its natural pointing. Your conscience-compass must not be influenced by greed or expediency. You must not trammel it. You must leave it free. The man who tampers with the needle of his conscience, who pulls it away from its natural love, and who tries to convince himself that there are other standards of right, other stars as reliable as the pole star of his character, and proposes to follow them in some questionable business, is a deluded fool who invites disaster.

Every little while I meet young men who dislike to tell me what their vocation is. They seem ashamed of what they are doing. One young man I met some time ago very reluctantly told me that he was a bartender in a large saloon. I asked him how long he had been there, and he said about six years. He said he hated the business; it was degrading; but that he was making pretty good money, and just as soon as he could get enough laid up, so that he could afford it, he was going to quit and go into something else. Now, this young man had been deceiving himself for years by thinking that he was doing pretty well, and that he would soon leave the business.

There is something very demoralizing to the whole nature in doing that against which the better self protests. An effort to reconcile the ideal with that which we cannot respect is fatal to all growth. This is the reason why men shrivel and shrink, instead of expanding, when they are out of place. A man does not grow when a large part of him is entering its protest against his work. A volunteer makes a better soldier than a drafted man.

A great many young men try to justify themselves and check inward protests by the perpetual self-suggestion that it is better to keep on, for the present, in questionable occupations, because the great financial reward will put them in position to do better later. This is a sort of sedative to the conscience to keep it quiet until they can afford to listen to it.

Do not deceive yourself by the expectation of making clean money in a dirty occupation. Do not deceive yourself, either, by thinking that you can elevate a bad business, or make it respectable. Many a man has been thus dragged down to his ruin. Some occupations are so demoralizing, brutalizing, and hardening that even a Lincoln could not make them respectable. If what you are doing is wrong, stop it. Have nothing to do with it. If you are in doubt, or if you suspect that you are warping your conscience, give yourself the benefit of the doubt. Take no chances with it. Leave it before it is too late.

Long familiarity with a bad business will make it seem right to you. If it is very profitable, it will at last hush your doubts and blunt your moral faculties. It will make you feel that there is compensation in pursuing it, at least until capital is accumulated for something else. Besides, the philosophy of habit is that every repetition of an act makes it more certain that it will be repeated again and again, quickly making the doer a slave. In spite of the protests of your weakened will, the trained nerves continue to repeat the acts even when you abhor them. What you at first choose, at last compels you. You are as irrevocably chained to your deeds as the atoms are chained by gravitation.

So, my friends, when you are thinking of engaging in an occupation which is a little questionable, and which does not get the complete consent of your faculties, do not forget this tremendous gripping power of habit, which, when you may wish to change, will pull like a giant to get you back into the old rut.

You have no right to choose an occupation which calls into play your inferior qualities, the lying, cunning, overreaching, scheming, long headed, underhanded qualities, those which covet and grasp and snatch, and never give, while all that is noblest in you shrivels and dies.

If you have already made a wrong choice, why should you remain in an occupation which does not have your unqualified approval, or in one of which you are ashamed, and in which you have to stretch your conscience every day to make deceitful statements and false representations to influence purchasers unduly; to induce them by a smooth manner and a lying tongue to do that which you know is not for their advantage, and for which you will reproach yourself afterwards?

Why should you desecrate your manhood and pervert your ability in a contemptible occupation, when there are so many clean, respectable vocations which are searching for your ability and hunting for your talent?

You say that it is hard for you to change. Of course it is hard to jog along in humdrum toil for the sake of being honest when acquaintances all around are getting rich by leaps and bounds. Of course it takes courage to refuse to bend the knee to questionable methods, lies, schemes, and fraud, when they are so generally used. Of course it takes courage to tell the exact truth when a little deception or a little departure from the right would bring great temporary gain. Of course it takes courage to refuse to be bribed when it could be covered up by a little specious mystification. Of course it takes courage to stand erect when by bowing and scraping to people with a pull you can get inside information which will make you win what you know others must lose. Of course it takes courage to determine never to put into your pocket a dirty dollar, a lying, deceitful dollar, a dollar that drips with human sorrow, or a dollar that has made some poor gullible wretch poorer, or has defeated another's cherished plans, or robbed him of ambition or education. But this is what character is for. This is what manhood means. This is what backbone and stamina were given us for, to stand for the right and oppose the wrong, no matter what the results.

Wear threadbare clothes, if necessary; live on one meal a day in a house with bare floors and bare walls, if you must ; but under no circumstances ever consent to prostitute your manhood, or to turn your ability to do an unclean thing. Dig trenches ; carry a hod ; work as a section-hand on a railroad ; shovel coal, anything rather than sacrifice your self-respect, blunt your sense of right and wrong, and shut yourself off forever from the true joy of living, and the approbation which comes only from the consciousness of doing your level best to reach the highest that is possible to you.

Do not choose that occupation which has the most money in it, the greatest promise of material reward, notoriety, or fame, even ; but choose that which will call out the man in you, and which will develop your greatest strength and symmetry of manhood, personal nobility. Manhood is greater than wealth and grander than fame. Personal nobility is greater than any calling, or any reward that it can bring.

X.

STAND FOR SOMETHING

THE greatest thing that can be said of a man, no matter how much he achieved, is that ***he has kept his record clean.***

Why is it that, in spite of the ravages of time, the reputation of Lincoln grows larger and his character means more to the world every year? It is because he kept his record clean, and never prostituted his ability nor gambled with his reputation.

Where, in all history, is there an example of a man who was merely rich, no matter how great his wealth, who exerted such a power for good, who was such a living force in civilization, as was this poor backwoods boy? What a powerful illustration of the fact that ***character*** is the greatest force in the world !

A man assumes importance and becomes a power in the world just as soon as it is found that he stands for something; that he is not for sale ; that he will not lease his manhood for salary, for any amount of money or for any influence or position ; that he will not l end his name to anything which he cannot indorse.

The trouble with so many men today is that they do not stand for anything outside their vocation. They may be well educated, well up in their specialties, may have a lot of expert knowledge, but they cannot be depended upon. There is some flaw in them which takes the edge off their virtue. They may be fairly honest, but you cannot bank on them.

It is not difficult to find a lawyer or a physician who knows a good deal, who is eminent in his profession ; but it is not so easy to find one who is a man before he is a lawyer or a physician; whose name is a synonym for all that is clean, reliable, solid, substantial. It is not difficult to find a good preacher ; but it is not so easy to find a real man, sterling manhood, back of the sermon. It is easy to find successful merchants, but not so easy to find men who put character above merchandise. What the world wants is men who have principle underlying their expertness principle under their law, their medicine, their business; men who stand for something outside of their offices and stores; who stand for something in their community; whose very presence carries weight.

Everywhere we see smart, clever, long headed, shrewd men, but how comparatively rare it is to find one whose record is as clean as a hound's tooth; who will not swerve from the right; who would rather fail than be a party to a questionable transaction !

Everywhere we see business men putting the stumbling-blocks of deception and dishonest methods right across their own pathway, tripping themselves up while trying to deceive others.

We see men worth millions of dollars filled with terror; trembling lest investigations may uncover things which will damn them in the public estimation ! We see them cowed before the law like whipped spaniels; catching at any straw that will save them from public disgrace

What a terrible thing to live in the limelight of popular favor, to be envied as rich and powerful, to be esteemed as honorable and straightforward, and yet to be conscious all the time of not being what the world thinks we are; to live in constant terror of discovery, in fear that something may happen to unmask us and show us up in our true light! But nothing can happen to injure seriously the man who lives four-square to the world; who has nothing to cover up, nothing to hide from his fellows; who lives a transparent, clean life, with never a fear of disclosures. If all of his material possessions are swept away from him, he knows that he has a monument in the hearts of his countrymen, in the affection and admiration of the people, and that nothing can happen to harm his real self because he has kept his record clean.

Mr. Roosevelt early resolved that, let what would come, whether he succeeded in what he undertook or failed, whether he made friends or enemies, he would not take chances with his good name he would part with everything else first; that he would never gamble with his reputation; that he would keep his record clean. His first ambition was to stand for something, to be a man. Before he was a politician or anything else the man must come first.

In his early career he had many opportunities to make a great deal of money by allying himself with crooked, sneaking, unscrupulous politicians. He had all sorts of opportunities for political graft. But crookedness never had any attraction for him. He refused to be a party to any political jobbery, any underhand business. He preferred to lose any position he was seeking, to let somebody else have it, if he must get smirched in the getting it. He would not touch a dollar, place, or preferment unless it came to him clean, with no trace of jobbery on it. Politicians who had an "ax to grind" knew it was no use to try to bribe him, or to influence him with promises of patronage, money, position, or power. Mr. Roosevelt knew perfectly well that he would make many mistakes and many enemies, but he resolved to carry himself in such a way that even his enemies should at least respect him for his honesty of purpose, and for his straightforward, "square-deal" methods. He resolved to keep his record clean, his name white, at all hazards. Everything else seemed unimportant in comparison.

In times like these the world especially needs such men as Mr. Roosevelt men who hew close to the chalk-line of right and hold the line plumb to truth; men who do not pander to public favor; men who make duty and truth their goal and go straight to their mark, turning neither to the right nor to the left, though a paradise tempt them.

Who can ever estimate how much his influence has done toward purging politics and elevating the American ideal. He has changed the view-point of many statesmen and politicians. He has shown them a new and a better way. He has made many of them ashamed of the old methods of grafting and selfish greed. He has held up a new ideal, shown them that unselfish service to their country is infinitely nobler than an ambition for self-aggrandizement. American patriotism has a higher meaning to-day, because of the example of this great American. Many young politicians and statesmen have adopted cleaner methods and higher aims because of his influence. There is no doubt that tens of thousands of young men in this country are cleaner in their lives, and more honest and ambitious to be good citizens, because here is a man who always stands for the "square deal," for civic righteousness, for American manhood.

Every man ought to feel that there is something in him that bribery cannot touch, that influence cannot buy ; something that is not for sale; something he would not sacrifice or tamper with for any price; something he would give his life for if necessary.

If a man stands for something worth while, compels recognition for himself alone, on account of his real worth, he is not dependent upon recommendations; upon fine clothes, a fine house, or a pull. He is his own best recommendation.

The young man who starts out with the resolution to make his character his capital, and to pledge his whole manhood for every obligation he enters into, will not be a failure, though he wins neither fame nor fortune. No man ever really does a great thing who loses his character in the process.

No substitute has ever yet been discovered for honesty. Multitudes of people have gone to the wall trying to find one. Our prisons are full of people who have attempted to substitute something else for it.

No man can really believe in himself when he is occupying a false position and wearing a mask; when the little monitor within him is constantly saying, " You know you are a fraud ; you are not the man you pretend to be." The consciousness of not being genuine, not being what others think him to be, robs a man of power, honeycombs the character, and destroys self-respect and self-confidence.

When Lincoln was asked to take the wrong side of a case he said, “I could not do it. All the time while talking to that jury I should be thinking, ' Lincoln, you're a liar, you're a liar and I believe I should forget myself and say it out loud."

Character as capital is very much underestimated by a great number of young men. They seem to put more emphasis upon smart' ness, shrewdness, long-headedness, cunning, influence, a pull, than upon downright honesty and integrity of character. Yet why do scores of concerns pay enormous sums for the use of the name of a man who, perhaps, has been dead for half a century or more ? It is because there is power in that name ; because there is character in it; because it stands for something; because it represents reliability and square dealing. Think of what the name of Tiffany, of Park and Til ford, or any of the great names which stand in the commercial world as solid and immovable as the rock of Gibraltar, are worth !

Does it not seem strange that young men who know these facts should try to build up a business on a foundation of cunning, scheming, and trickery, instead of building on the solid rock of character, reliability, and manhood? Is it not remarkable that so many men should work so hard to establish a business on an unreliable, flimsy foundation, instead of building upon the solid masonry of honest goods, square dealing, reliability?

A name is worth everything until it is questioned; but when suspicion clings to it, it is worth nothing. There is nothing in this world that will take the place of character. There is no policy in the world, to say nothing of the right or wrong of it, that compares with honesty and square dealing.

In spite of, or because of, all the crookedness and dishonesty that is being uncovered, of all the scoundrels that are being unmasked, integrity is the biggest word in the business world to-day. There never was a time in all history when it was so big, and it is growing bigger. There never was a time when character meant so much in business ; when it stood for so much everywhere as it does to-day.

There was a time when the man who was the shrewdest and sharpest and cunningest in taking advantage of others got the biggest salary; but to-day the man at the other end of the bargain is looming up as never before.

Nathan Straus, when asked the secret of the great success of his firm, said it was their treatment of the man at the other end of the bargain. He said they could not afford to make enemies; they could not afford to displease or to take advantage of customers, or to give them reason to think that they had been unfairly dealt with, that, in the long run, the man who gave the squarest deal to the man at the other end of the bargain would get ahead fastest.

There are merchants who have made great fortunes, but who do not carry weight among their fellow men because they have dealt all their lives with inferiority. They have lived with shoddy and shams so long that the suggestion has been held in their minds until their whole standards of life have been lowered; their ideals have shrunken; their characters have partaken of the quality of their business.

Contrast these men with the men who stood for half a century or more at the head of solid houses, substantial institutions ; men who have always stood for quality in everything; who have surrounded themselves not only with ability but with men and women of character.

We instinctively believe in character. We admire people who stand for something; who are centered in truth and honesty. It is not necessary that they agree with us. We admire them for their strength, the honesty of their opinions, the inflexibility of their principles.

The late Carl Schurz was a strong man and antagonized many people. He changed his political views very often; but even his worst enemies knew there was one thing he would never go back on, friends or no friends, party or no party and that was his devotion to principle as he saw it. There was no parleying with his convictions. He could stand alone, if necessary, with all the world against him. His inconsistencies, his many changes in parties and politics, could not destroy the universal admiration for the man who stood for his convictions. Although he escaped from a German prison and fled his country, where he had been arrested on account of his revolutionary principles when but a mere youth, Emperor William the First had such a profound respect for his honesty of purpose and his strength of character that he invited him to return to Germany and visit him, gave him a public dinner, and paid him great tribute.

Who can estimate the influence of President Eliot in enriching and uplifting our national ideas and standards through the thousands of students who go out from Harvard University? The tremendous force and nobility of character of Phillips Brooks raised every one who came within his influence to higher levels. His great earnestness in trying to lead people up to his lofty ideals swept everything before it. One could not help feeling while listening to him and watching him th*at there* was a mighty triumph of character, a grand expression of superb manhood. Such men as these increase our faith in the race ; in the possibilities of the grandeur of the coming man. We are prouder of our country because of such standards.

It is the ideal that determines the direction of the life. And what a grand sight, what an inspiration, are those men who sacrifice the dollar to the ideal !

The principles by which the problem of success is solved are right and justice, honesty and integrity ; and just in proportion as a man deviates from these principles he falls short of solving his problem.

It is true that he may reach *something.* He may get money, but is that success ? The thief gets money, but does he succeed? Is it any honester to steal by means of a long head than by means of a long arm? It is very much more dishonest, because the victim is deceived and then robbed a double crime.

We often receive letters which read like this:

"I am getting a good salary ; but I do not feel right about it, somehow. I cannot still the voice within me that says, 'Wrong, wrong,' to what I am doing." "

" Leave it, leave it," we always say to the writers of these letters. "Do not stay in a questionable occupation, no matter what inducement it offers. Its false light will land you on the rocks if you follow it. It is demoralizing to the mental faculties, paralyzing to the character, to do a thing which one's conscience forbids."

"Tell the employer who expects you to do questionable things that you cannot work for him unless you can put the trademark of your manhood, the stamp of your integrity, upon everything you do. Tell him that if the highest thing in you cannot bring success, surely the lowest cannot. You cannot afford to sell the best thing in you, your honor, your manhood, to a dishonest man or a lying institution. You should regard even the suggestion that you might sell out for a consideration as an insult.

Resolve that you will not be paid for being something less than a man; that you will not lease your ability, your education, your inventiveness, your self-respect, for salary, to do a man's lying for him; either in writing advertisements, selling goods, or in any other capacity.

Resolve that, whatever your vocation, you are going to stand for something ; that you are not going to be *merely* a lawyer, a physician, a merchant, a clerk, a farmer, a congressman, or a man who carries a big money-bag; but that you are going to be a *man* first, last, and all the time.

XI.

HAPPY? IF NOT, WHY NOT?

WE have seen many painful examples during the past few months of the failure of wealth to produce happiness. We have seen that a fortune without a man behind it does not stand for much. The X-rays of public investigation have revealed some ghastly spectacles.

Of a number of rich men who were in positions of great responsibility and trust at the beginning of the recent financial panic, some have committed suicide, others have died from the effects of the disgrace which they had brought upon themselves and their families, and still others have suffered tortures, not so much because of their wrongdoings, as from the fear of disclosure.

A few months ago, these men were supposed to possess the things which make men happy. They had what all the world is seeking so strenuously money. They lived in palatial homes and were surrounded with luxuries, and yet, the moment misfortune came, what they called "happiness" fled as though it had the wings of a bird.

These men felt secure because they had that which most people are struggling so hard to get. They had supposed themselves so firmly intrenched in the wherewithal of life, so buttressed by their "solid " investments, that nothing could shake them. But, almost in the twinkling of an eye, their foundations slipped from under them, their reputations vanished, and, instead of being the big men they thought they were, they not only found that they were nobodies, but also that their " happiness " had flown with their reputations. Happiness is not such a transient visitor as that. If these men had had the genuine article, no panic could have shaken it, no fire burned it out, no ocean swallowed it up. Real happiness is not a fluttering, fly-away unreality. It is not superficial. It does not live in things. It does not depend upon money. It inheres in character, in personality. It consists in facing life the right way, and no one who faces it the wrong way, no matter how much money he may have, can ever be happy.

The trouble with many of the men who went down in the panic was that they put the emphasis upon the wrong thing.

Man is built upon the plan of honesty, of rectitude the divine plan. When he perverts his nature by trying to express dishonesty, chicanery, and cunning, of course he cannot be happy. The very essence of happiness is honesty, sincerity, truthfulness. He who would have real happiness for his companion must be clean, straightforward, and sincere. The moment he departs from the right she will take wings and fly away.

What a pitiable thing it is to see the human race chasing the dollar material things trying to extract happiness, to squeeze joy, out of money alone! How little people realize that the very thing they are hunting lives in themselves or nowhere ; that if they do not take happiness with them they may hunt the earth over without finding it. Happiness is a condition of mind. It is a fundamental principle, and he who does not understand the principle cannot possibly be happy.

All the misery and the crime of the world rest upon the failure of human beings to understand the principle that no man can really be happy until he harmonizes with the best thing in him, with the divine, and not with the brute. No one can be happy who tries to harmonize his life with his animal instincts. The God (the good) in him is the only possible thing that can make him happy.

Real happiness cannot be bribed by anything sordid or low. Nothing mean or unworthy appeals to it. There is no affinity between them. Founded upon principle, it is as scientific as the laws of mathematics, and he who works his problem correctly will get the happiness answer.

There is only one way to secure the correct answer to a mathematical problem; and that is to work in harmony with mathematical laws. It would not matter if half the world believed there was some other way to get the answer, it would never come until the law was followed with the utmost exactitude. It does not matter that the great majority of the human race believe there is some other way of reaching the happiness goal. The fact that they are discontented, restless, and unhappy, shows that they are not working their problem scientifically.

We are all conscious that there is another man inside of us; that there accompanies us through life a divine, silent messenger that other, higher, better self which speaks from the depths of our nature and which gives its consent, its "Amen," to every right action, and condemns every wrong one.

Men and women in all times have tried to bribe this constant monitor; to purchase its approval; to silence it in nervous excitement; to drown it in vicious pleasure, with drink and with drugs but all in vain. Men in every age have disregarded its warning; have tried in every possible way to get away from its tormenting reproofs when they have done wrong ; but no amount of dissipation or excitement has ever been able to silence its voice. It always continues to give its unbiased, unbribed approval or disapproval to whatever we do.

There is nothing in which people deceive themselves so much as in the pursuit of happiness. There is only one way to find it that is, by obeying the laws upon which we are built. We are constructed along the lines of truth and justice, and we cannot reach felicity by disobeying these, the very laws of our nature. So long as we continue to do evil, to get money by unfair means by robbing others or taking advantage of them so long as our ambition is to get rich anyway, we can never attain true happiness, because we are going in the wrong direction. We are introducing discord into our natures ; encouraging the very opposite to what we are seeking.

It is just as impossible for a person to reach the normal state of harmony while he is practicing selfish, grasping methods, as it is to produce harmony in an orchestra with instruments that are all jangled and out of tune. To be happy, we must be in tune with the Infinite within us, in harmony with our better selves. There is no way to get around it.

The idea that we can practice wrong in our vocations, in our dealings with men, or in our pleasures, and then periodically seek forgive- ness in our prayers or through our churches the idea that a man can do wrong and be for- given without remedying the wrong, or without forsaking the sin, has done more harm than almost any other thing in civilization. A clear conscience, a clean life, the elimination of selfishness, jealousy, envy, and hatred, are necessary to all ***high*** enjoyment.

One trouble with many of us is that we try to make happiness too complicated an affair. But happiness really flees from complication, ceremony, and pretense. Nature has fixed her everlasting edict against complicated living. You can never force pleasure it must be natural ; it must come from sane living.

Real happiness is so simple that most people do not recognize it. They think it comes from doing something on a big scale, from a big fortune, or from some great achievement, when, in fact, it is derived from the simplest, the quietest, the most unpretentious things in the world.

Our great problem is to fill each day so full of sunshine, of plain living and high thinking, that there can be no commonness or unhappiness in our lives. Little kindnesses, pleasant words, and helps by the way ; trifling courtesies and encouragements; duties faithfully done, unselfish service, work that we enjoy; friendships, love, and affection all these are simple things, yet they are what constitute happiness.

The great sanitariums, the noted springs of the world, are crowded with rich people, sent there by their physicians to get rid of the effects of complicated living. They tried to force their pleasures and came to grief.

Not long ago, I dined in the home of a very rich man, and it took two hours and a half to serve the dinner. There were thirteen courses, made up of the richest kinds of food, and many of them absolutely incompatible with one another. In addition to this, there were seven kinds of wine ! Think of any one being healthy or happy living upon such a diet!

What are the enjoyments of the average rich? Is there anything more vapid, insipid, unsatisfying than the chasing after that indefinite, mysterious something which they call happiness ; that will-o'-the-wisp which is always beckoning them on, but ever eluding their grasp; that rainbow which recedes as they approach? They may enjoy the titillation of the nerves for a moment, the temporary excitement and exhilaration which come from even vicious pleasures. But what of it all ? It is only animal enjoyment. Nothing but regret, disappointment, and disgust follow.

There is within every normal person a strong desire to do something and to be something in the world ; and every idler knows that he is violating the fundamental demand of his nature; that he is really cheating himself out of a very sacred prize, the getting of which would mean more to him than everything else in the world. I have talked with idle rich young men who said they knew that it was all wrong for them to refuse to do their part of the world's work; that it was a mistake for them not to enter into the activities of life and struggle for a prize which the Creator had fitted them to take; but that the paralyzing effect of not being obliged to work had undermined their inclination.

Recently a rich young man was asked why he did not work. " I do not have to," he said. " Do not have to " has ruined more young men than almost anything else. The fact is, Nature never made any provision for the idle man. Vigorous activity is the law of life ; it is the saving grace, the only thing that can keep a human being from retrograding. Activity along the line of one's highest ambition is the normal state of man, and he who tries to evade it pays the penalty in deterioration of faculty, in paralysis of efficiency. Do not flatter yourself that you can be really happy unless you are useful. Happiness and usefulness were born twins. To separate them is fatal.

It is as impossible for a human being to be happy who is habitually idle as it is for a fine chronometer to be normal when not running. The highest happiness is the feeling of well-being which comes to one who is actively employed in doing what he was made to do; carrying out the great life-purpose patterned in his individual bent. The practical fulfilling of the life-purpose is to man what the actual running and keeping time are to the watch. Without action both are meaningless.

There is no tonic like that which comes from doing things worth while. There is no happiness like that which comes from doing our level best every day, everywhere; no satisfaction like that which comes from stamping our superiority, putting our royal trade-mark, upon everything which goes through our hands.

Man was made to do things. Nothing else can take the place of achievement in his life. Real happiness without achievement of some worthy aim is unthinkable. One of the greatest satisfactions in this world is the feeling of enlargement, of growth, of stretching upward and onward. No pleasure can surpass that which comes from the consciousness of feeling one's horizon of ignorance being pushed farther and farther away of making headway in the world of not only getting on, but also of getting up.

Happiness is incompatible with stagnation. A man must feel his expanding power lifting, tugging away at a lofty purpose, or he will miss the joy of living.

The discords, the bickerings, and divorces; the breaking up of rich homes, and the resorting to all sorts of silly devices by many rich people in their pursuit of happiness, prove that it does not dwell within them ; that happiness does not abide with low ideals, with selfishness, idleness, and discord. It is a friend of harmony ; of truth and beauty ; of affection and simplicity.

Multitudes of men have made fortunes, but have murdered their capacity for enjoyment in the process. How often we hear the remark, "He has the money, but cannot enjoy it."

A man can have no greater delusion than that he can spend the best years of his life coining all of his energies into dollars, neglecting his home, sacrificing friendships, self- improvement, and everything else that is really worth while, for money, and yet find happiness at the end

If a man coins his ability, his opportunities into dollars, and during all the years he is accumulating wealth neglects the cultivation of the only faculties which are capable of appreciating the highest happiness, he cannot effectively revive his atrophied brain cells. His enjoyment, after he makes his money, must come from the exercise of the same faculties which he has employed in making it. He cannot undo the results of a life habit after he retires from business.

If you have not kept alive your ability to appreciate the beautiful, the good, and the true, you will be as surprised to find that it has left you as Darwin was when, in middle life, he discovered all at once that he had lost his power to appreciate Shakespeare and music.

We ought to be able to get a good living, even to make fortunes, and yet have a jolly good time every day of our lives. This idea of being a slave most of the time, and of only occasionally enjoying a holiday, is all wrong. Every day should be a holiday, a day of joy and gladness, a day of supreme happiness; and it would be, if we lived sanely, if we knew the secret of right thinking and normal living.

Isn't it strange that so few people ever think of making happiness a daily duty; that they should put this everlasting emphasis upon their vocations, on money making, and let the thing for which they really live come incidentally or without planning ? The making of a life should be emphasized infinitely more than the making of a living.

Few people ever learn the art of enjoying the little things of life as they go along. Yet it is the little, everyday enjoyments and satisfactions that count most in a lifetime. Almost every person I know is living in anticipation, not in reality. He is not actually living the life he has always looked forward to, or expected to attain; but is just getting ready to live, just getting ready to enjoy it. When he gets a little more money, a little better house, a little more of the comforts of life, a little more leisure, a little more freedom from responsibility, he will then be ready to enjoy life.

It is a rare thing to find a person who can truthfully say : " I am really living. This is the life I have been striving for, the life that I have looked forward to as being as near my ideal as I am likely to find in this world."

It is a great thing so to cultivate the art of happiness that we can get pleasure out of the common experiences of every day. The happiness habit is just as necessary to our best welfare as the work habit, or the honesty or square-dealing habit.

No one can do his best, his highest work, who is not perfectly normal, and happiness it a fundamental necessity of our being. It is an indication of health, of sanity, of harmony, The opposite is a symptom of disease, of abnormality. There are plenty of evidences in the human economy that we were intended for happiness, that it is our normal condition ; that suffering, unhappiness, discontent, are absolutely foreign and abnormal to our natures.

There is no doubt that our life was intended to be one grand, sweet song. We are built upon the plan of harmony, and every form of discord is abnormal. There is something wrong when any human being in this world, tuned to infinite harmonies and beauties that are unspeakable, is unhappy and discontented.

One of the most inexplicable mysteries that has ever puzzled the selfish rich is their failure to find happiness where they had expected to find it. The bitterest disappointment that comes to people who have made fortunes is that the wealth did not bring the happiness which it promised, or anything like it. They find that the affections do not feed on material things, that the heart would starve in the midst of the greatest luxuries alone. They find that, while money can do many things, it has little power to satisfy the heart yearnings, the heart hunger. How many women there are in palatial homes in this country who are starving for happiness and who would gladly exchange all their luxuries for the love of a good man, even if he had not a dollar in the world !

No selfish life can ever be happy. I am acquainted with a self-made man who has made a fortune, who tells me that the greatest enigma and disappointment of his life lie in the fact that, although he has made millions, he is not happy. He says that somehow he has never been able to make many friends; that people avoid him ; that he has never been able to get the confidence of others to any very great extent, and that he is not popular even among his own neighbors. He cannot understand why he is not happy, for, he tells me, he has tried very hard to find happiness.

The trouble with him is that he has always done everything with reference to himself. He did not mean to be selfish; but the whole passion of his life has been to make money, because he thought that would bring everything else that is desirable. He has chosen his friends for their ability to advance his interests, and has considered every step in life with reference to the effect it would have upon him. " What is there in it for me ? " seems to have been the interrogation point in his life.

Now, happiness is a reflection, an echo, a part of what we do and think. It does not depend upon our material possessions. Thoreau's cabin, at Walden Pond, cost only thirty-one dollars, and yet Thoreau was rich and happy because he had a rich mind.

It is as impossible for the selfish, greedy, grasping thought, the thought always centered upon one's own interest, to produce a happy state of mind as it is for thistle seeds to produce wheat. But if we sow helpfulness, kindness, unselfishness, we shall reap a harvest of satisfaction, harmony, and happiness. Selfishness and real happiness never go together. They are fatally antagonistic.

An inordinate ambition, a desire to get ahead of others, a mania to keep up appearances at all hazards, whether we can afford it or not, all these things feed selfishness, that corrosive acid which eats away our possible enjoyment and destroys the very sources of happiness. The devouring ambition to get ahead of others in money making, to outshine others socially, develops a sordid, grasping disposition which is the bane of happiness. No man with greed developed big within him can be happy. Neither contentment, satisfaction, serenity, affection, nor any other member of the happiness family can exist in the presence of greed.

It is as impossible for a man who has been dishonest, who has gotten his wealth by crushing others, and by taking advantage of them, to be happy as it is for a person really to enjoy himself while walking with pebbles in his shoes, or while constantly being nettled with pin pricks.

No man can be happy who is conscious of being a drone, of shirking his share in the great world's work, who knows that he is taking all the good things he can get hold of in life's great granary, put there by the toilers, and is putting nothing back.

A debauched mind that has departed from the principles of right thinking and right living has incapacitated itself for real enjoyment.

The only way to get the happiness that is worth while is to live a straight, clean, pure, honest, useful life. There is no power in the universe that can make a human being happy along any other lines.

Straightforward, honest work, a determined endeavor to do one's best, an earnest desire to scatter flowers instead of thorns, to make other people a little better off, a little happier because of our existence, these are the only recipes for real happiness.

No man can be happy when he despises his own acts, when he has any consciousness of wrong, whether of motive or act. No man can be happy when he harbors thoughts of revenge, jealousy, envy, or hatred. He must have a clean heart, and a clean conscience, or no amount of money or excitement can make him happy.

XII.

ORIGINALITY

NO human being ever yet made a success trying to be somebody else, even if that person was a success. Success cannot be copied cannot be successfully imitated. It is an original force an individual creation. Every man will be a failure just in proportion as he gets away from himself and tries to be somebody else and to express somebody else instead of himself. Power comes from within or from nowhere. Be yourself. Listen to the voice within. There is room for improvement in every profession, in every trade, and in every business. The world wants men who can do things in new and better ways. Don't think, because your plan or idea has no precedent, or because you are young and inexperienced, that you will not get a hearing. The man who has anything new and valuable to give to the world will be listened to and will be followed. The man of strong individuality, who dares to think his own thought and originate his own method, who is not afraid to be himself, and is not a copy of someone else, quickly gets recognition. Nothing else will attract the attention of an employer or the rest of the world so quickly as originality and unique ways of doing things, especially if they are effective.

Blaze your own way, make your own path, or you will never make any impression on the world. It is striking originality that attracts attention. The world admires the man who has the courage to lift his head above the crowd, who dares to step to the front and declare himself. Never before was originality so much at a premium. The world makes way for the man with an idea. It is the thinker, the man with original ideas and new and upto date methods, who is the real productive force in a community. He is wanted everywhere. But there is very little demand for human machines.

The world is full of followers, leaners, and taggers, who are willing to walk in old trails, and to have their thinking done for them ; but it is seeking the man with original force, who leaves the beaten track and pushes into new fields, the physician who departs from the precedent of those who have gone before him, the lawyer who conducts his case in an original way, the teacher who brings new ideas and methods into the schoolroom, and the clergyman who has the courage to proclaim the message which God has given to him, not that given to some other man who has put it into a book. The world wants preachers who get their sermons out of life, not out of a library.

There are a thousand people who will do faithfully what they are told, to one who can lay out a programme or execute it; a thousand who can only follow, to one who can lead. It is a rare thing to find a young man who has the power of initiative and the ability to put a thing through with the force of originality.

What ever your work in life, do not follow others. Do not imitate. Do not do things just as everybody else has done them before, but in new, ingenious ways. Show the people in your specialty that precedents do not cut much of a figure with you, and that you will make your own programme. Resolve that, whether you accomplish much or little in the world, it shall be original your own. Do not be afraid to assert yourself in a bold individual way. Originality is power, life; imitation is death. Do not be afraid to let yourself out. You grow by being original, never by copying ; by leading, never by following. Resolve that you will be a man of ideas, always on the lookout for improvement. Think to some purpose. There is always a place for an original man.

There is nothing else which will kill the creative faculty and paralyze growth more quickly than following precedents in everything, and doing everything in the same old way. I have known progressive young men to stop growing, become hopelessly rutty, and lose all their progressiveness by going into their fathers' stores, factories, or places of business, where everything was done in the same old-fashioned way, and precedents were followed in everything. They lost all expansiveness. There was no motive for reaching out for the new and the original, because their fathers would not change. I have seen splendid fellows, who might have become great and grand men, shrivel to pygmies in their fathers' ruts.

How many of our business houses are weighted down with machinery, old, antiquated methods, ponderous bookkeeping, and out-of-date appliances, when new devices, or new methods with short-cut ways of doing things would enable them to economize greatly on room and to get along with much less help ; but they cling to the old with a fatal tenacity.

This is why so many old concerns, which have been strong and powerful for generations, gradually shrink, shrivel, get into ruts, and fail, while their newer competitors, the bright young men who have gone out from these houses, do things in a new way, adopt up-to-date methods, keep up with the times, and go on to greater success.

There is a great advertising quality in originality, or uniqueness. The man who does business like the great majority of men, although he may have superior ability, does not attract much attention. But if he makes his own path, adopts original and progressive methods, puts his specialty in a class by itself, and attracts attention, everybody who patronizes him is a traveling advertisement for him.

There is a specialty store in Boston whose progressive proprietors make a study of original ways of doing everything. For example, all change is given in brand new money, direct from the United States treasury or mint. This does not cost much, and causes but little trouble, yet it is a very shrewd advertisement. It is especially attractive to women and children, and has brought a great deal of trade. Aside from the danger of handling old, soiled money, which has been no one knows where, it gives a sense of pleasure to handle new, crisp bills, and brand new, bright coins. This is only one of the many unique methods this concern adopts.

People flock to the most up-to-date establishments, for they know that the newest styles, the latest and freshest goods, the greatest variety, the best display of taste, and the most appropriate things are to be found there. It is well known that those up-to-date houses pay the largest salaries and have the best buyers.

There is a hotel in New York which needs no advertising. It is one of the institutions which people visit out of interest, and they are always talking about it. Other things being equal, they will patronize it. If they cannot afford to have rooms there, they will go there to dine, to see the fashions, and prominent people. The amount of free advertising which this hotel has had, in addition to what, perhaps, other first-class hotels get, would probably have cost, if paid for, half as much as the hotel is worth.

The same is true in every line of endeavor. It is the newest and the most up-to-date concern, that has the latest devices and the freshest, and most original ideas, that draws the people. Do not, however, make the mistake of thinking that if you simply do things in new ways you will necessarily be successful. It is effective originality that counts. There are thousands of men who are always chasing new ideas, new ways of doing things, who never accomplish anything of note, because they are not effective, not practical. I know a man who adopts every new device that comes along, and has thus practically run through a large estate left him, because he did not have the judgment or the sagacity to select really effective devices or methods in the management of his affairs.

The shrewdest thing a young man can do to say nothing of the influence upon his character is to put the greatest possible originality and the highest possible excellence into everything he does; to make a resolution, at the very outset of his career, to stamp his individuality upon everything that goes out of his hands, and to determine that everything he does shall have the imprint of his character upon it as a trade-mark of the highest and best that is in him. If he does this, he will not require a large amount of capital to start a business, and to advertise it. His greatest resources will be in himself. Originality is the best substitute for advertising, as well as the best thing to advertise, if quality goes with it. Some men are absolutely afraid to do things in a new way. They must follow some- body else. "What was good enough for my father and grandfather is good enough for me " seems to be their motto. They cannot see any reason for changing. They must have a precedent for everything or they reject it. They cannot appreciate a new idea or a new way of doing things. They think there must be something the matter with it if it has not been used before. They have a peculiar love for the old ; the antique appeals to them. They think the value of things lies in their age. These people with hide-bound intellects stand in the way of progress. Every town has these "precedent men" in the same old-sized stores with the same old, out-of-date show-windows, the same methods of displaying goods, the same old, cumbersome systems in the countin groom. They are progresspro of. New ideas frighten them. The precedent man is always nonplussed, embarrassed by anything new, or when confronted with a condition which requires something original. He must get hold of something which has been used before, or he is powerless.

Many people think it is unfortunate to be unlike others in their personalities. They are always afraid of being thought peculiar, or eccentric. Yet the Creator never made two things alike, nor any two people alike. Nature breaks her mold at every new birth. Great characters always have strong individuality and originality, characteristics which mark them from the crowd. To be eccentric is not to be weak, but more often it is a sign of strength. Lincoln had eccentricities, but they were inseparable from his great character. Eccentricities which do not make a person disagreeable or repulsive are often advantageous rather than disadvantageous.

What is more monotonous than a dead level, insipid character, that has no strongly marked features which individualize it? We all love a great nature, a strong, vigorous, rugged personality, which impresses us with power something colossal which looms above us and inspires us with awe and admiration, such as we feel when standing under some mighty mountain cliff towering above us into the clouds. We do not wish the rugged crags smoothed off. They add to the peak's sublimity. They suggest majesty and power. Why should we want to plane off the eccentricities of a great character, or the individuality which characterizes him and distinguishes him from all others ?

We believe in the original man or woman who does not remind us of others, who makes a new, strong, vigorous, and lasting impression upon us, who does not imitate, or follow, who makes his own programme, who acts upon his own judgment, who leans upon nobody, and who does not ask advice, but acts fearlessly, boldly, independently. We know there is force there that can do things that can achieve a reserve power that makes its possessor a master. Fearlessness is a quality absolutely necessary to great achievement, courage always accompanies force. It is a marked quality of the original man. Imitators are timid, weak.

Do not be afraid of being original. Be an independent, self-reliant, new man, not just one more individual in the world. Do not try to be a copy of your grandfather, your father, or your neighbor. That is as foolish as for a violet to try to be like a rose, or for a daisy to ape a sunflower. Nature has given each a peculiar equipment for its purpose. Every man is born to do a certain work in an original way. If he tries to copy some other man, or to do some other man's work, he will be an abortion, a misfit, a failure.

Do not imitate even your heroes. Scores of young clergymen attempted to make their reputations by imitating Beecher. They copied his voice and conversation, and imitated his gestures and his habits, but they fell as far short of the great man's power as the chromo falls short of the masterpiece. Where are those hundreds of imitators now? Not one of them has ever made any stir in the world. The world puts its ban upon all imitations. It despises a man who tags on to somebody else, leans or imitates. He is always classed as a weakling, without force, power, or individuality.

We hear a great deal about the dangers of the one man power in our great corporations. People say that they should be managed by large committees, or boards of directors ; that too much power should not be put into the hands of one man. But there is one original, dominating character in every committee, on every board of directors, who towers above all the others and ultimately rules. It is impossible to get away from the domination of a strong, original, forceful character.

Just be yourself. The consciousness that you are not another in the slightest degree, that there is no suggestion of being a copy of somebody else about you, is a great power in itself. It increases your confidence. The very reputation of being original buttresses you in any community. It helps you to have people say, after talking with you, " There, I met an original man, to-day, who did not even remind me of anybody else I have ever seen." It is refreshing to talk with a man who never reminds you of others, who uses no cant, who is not the slave of precedent, who walks on his own legs, who has no use for crutches, and who never leans, a man of force, who radiates power.

Why try to be somebody else? To be yourself, or to express yourself with originality and power, is the greatest thing you can do. You cannot be another if you try. It only makes you unnatural and ridiculous, and robs you of the power which comes from self-expression, from being yourself. The more you differ from another man by nature, the more ridiculous you will make yourself by attempting to imitate him. Real strength inheres in personality.

XIII.

HAD MONEY BUT LOST IT

PROMINENT New York lawyer of wide experience says that, in his opinion, ninety-nine out of every hundred of those who make money or inherit it, lose it, sooner or later.

What a spectacle, everywhere in this land of plenty, of inexhaustible resources and unlimited opportunity, where every man ought to be a king, to see God's noblemen living like European peasants because they never learned to do business in a business way!

How many thousands of good, honest men and women there are in this country who have worked very hard and made all sorts of sacrifices of comfort and luxury in order to lay up something for the future, and yet have reached middle life or later without having anything to show for it; many of them, indeed, finding themselves without a home or any probability of getting one, without property or a cent of money laid by for sickness, for the inevitable emergency, or for their declining years!

It seems incredible that a strong, sturdy, self-made man, who has had to fight his way up from poverty, and who feels the backache in every dollar he has earned, should let his savings slip through his fingers in the most foolish investments, with scarcely any investigation, often sending his money thousands of miles away to people he has never seen, and about whom he knows practically nothing, except through an advertisement which has attracted his attention, or through the wiles of some smooth, unprincipled promoter.

Great numbers of vast fortunes in this country have been and are being built up on the very ignorance of the masses in regard to business methods. The schemers bank on it that it is easy to swindle people who do not know how to protect their property. They thrive on the ignorance of their fellows. They know that a shrewd advertisement, a cunningly worded circular, a hypnotic appeal will bring the hard earnings of these unsuspecting people out of hiding-places into their own coffers.

For the sake of your home, for the protection of your hard earnings, for your peace of mind, your self-respect, your self-confidence, whatever else you do, do not neglect a good, solid business training, and get it as early in life as possible. It will save you from many a fall, from a thousand embarrassments, and perhaps from the humiliation of being compelled to face your wife and children and confess that you have been a failure. It may spare you the mortification of having to move from a good home to a poor one, of seeing your property slip out of your hands, and of having to acknowledge your weakness and your lack of foresight and thoughtfulness, or it may prevent your being made the dupe of sharpers.

Many men who once had good stores of their own, are working as clerks, floor-walkers, or superintendents of departments in other people's stores, just because they risked and lost everything in some venture. As they now have others depending on them, they do not dare to take the risks which they took in young manhood to get a new start, and so they struggle along in mediocre positions, still mocked with ambitions which they have no chance to gratify.

How many inventors and discoverers have fought the fight of desperation amidst poverty and deprivation for years and years, and have succeeded in giving the world that which helps to emancipate man from drudgery and to ameliorate the hard conditions of civilization, and yet have allowed others to snatch their victories away from them and leave them penniless, just because they did not know how to protect themselves!

Thousands of people who were once in easy circumstances are living in poverty and wretchedness to-day because they failed to put an understanding or an agreement in writing, or to do business in a business way. Families have been turned, penniless, out of house and home, because they trusted to a relative or a friend to " do what was right " by them, without making a hard and fast, practical business arrangement with him.

It does not matter how honest people are, they may forget, and it is so easy for misunderstandings to arise that it is never safe to leave anything of importance to a mere oral statement. Reduce it to writing.

It costs but little, in time or money, and when all parties interested are agreed, that is the best time to formulate the agreement in exact terms. This will often save lawsuits, bitterness, and alienations. How many friendships have been broken because understandings were not put in writing! Thousands of cases are in the courts to-day for this reason, and a large part of lawyers' incomes is derived from them.

Many people have a foolish idea that others, especially friends or relatives, will be sensitive and think their honesty questioned if they are asked to put their proposition, or agreement, or understanding in writing. It is not a question of confidence. It is a question of business, and business should be done in a business way, so that in case of death, or some other unforeseen event, every possibility of complication or misunderstanding will be eliminated. The very people you may think will be sensitive or offended because you are so exacting will really think more of you for your straightforward business methods and your carefulness in avoiding misunderstanding.

Many a cultured girl has been thrown suddenly on her own resources by the failure or the death of her father, and has found herself wholly incapable of administering his affairs or of earning a living. Many women, their husbands having died suddenly, are left with large business responsibilities, which they are utterly unfit to assume. They are at the mercy of designing lawyers or dishonest business men, who well know that they are mere babies in their hands when it comes to important transactions.

Business talent is as rare as a talent for mathematics. We find boys and girls turned out of school and college full of theories, and of all sorts of knowledge or smatterings of knowledge, but without the ability to protect themselves from human thieves who are trying to get something for nothing. No girl or boy should be allowed to graduate, especially from any of the higher institutions, without being well grounded in practical business methods. Parents who send their children out in life, without seeing that they are well versed in ordinary business principles, do them an incalculable injustice.

I have heard a young woman boast that she did not know anything about money matters, and had no desire to. She said that she had no idea of the value of a dollar, that she could spend all the money she could get, but that it was distasteful to her to discuss economy. Many such women object to any common-sense consideration of the financial question. They think it is not necessary for them to know anything about money from the purely business point of view, as they consider that phase of life belongs wholly to their fathers or brothers or husbands.

An instructive example of the result of such spirit and ignorance I found in a lady who had lost her property through a lack of business knowledge. She told me that she knew nothing whatever about business. She had never known the value of money. Her husband died and left her with a large property, and it was her custom to sign any paper or document that her lawyer or agents presented to her, usually without reading. The people who had charge of her property knew that she knew nothing about business and took advantage of her ignorance. They got her property away from her, and she did not have enough left even to conduct a legal fight to get it back.

Thousands of girls are sent out into the world with what is called finished educations, who cannot even give a proper receipt for money, to say nothing of drawing a promissory note, a draft or a bill, or understanding the significance and importance of business contracts. Such a woman presented a check for payment to the paying teller of her bank.

He passed it back to her with the request that she be kind enough to indorse it. The lady wrote on the back of the check," I have done business with this bank for many years, and I believe it to be all right. Mrs. James B. Brown."

A society woman in "New York presented a check for payment at a bank, and the teller told her that it was not signed. " Oh, do they have to be signed ? " she responded. " What an awful lot of red tape there is about the banking business."

I know of a lady whose husband made a deposit for her in a bank and gave her a check book so that she could pay her bills without calling on him for money. One day she received a notice from the bank that her account was overdrawn. She went to the bank and told the teller that there must be a mistake about it, because she still had a lot of checks left in her book. She knew so little about business methods that she thought she could keep drawing any amount until the checks were all gone.

This sounds ridiculous and almost incredible, yet the very girl who laughs at it may make even more absurd blunders. Many an accomplished woman, when given a pen and asked to sign an important document drawn up by an attorney or a long-headed business man, will sign it without reading it or even asking to be informed of its contents, only to learn afterwards by disastrous results that she has signed away her property and turned herself out of her home. Only a short time ago I read of a lady who had won a suit involving about $20,000. New evidence, however, was brought forward, which caused the court immediately to reverse its decision. It was proved that the lady had sworn falsely. She was perfectly innocent of any such intention, but she had sworn that she had never signed her name to a certain document. The document was produced, and, to her utter astonishment, she saw her signature affixed to it. She acknowledged at once that the signature was hers, although she had just sworn that she had never signed the paper in question. It appeared that, during her husband's lifetime, whenever papers were to be signed, he told her where to write her name, and she did as she was told, without having the slightest idea of the contents of the papers.

Many people have come to grief by giving full power of attorney to their lawyer or business agent. Very few impractical people, especially women, understand the significance of a full power of attorney, which authorizes the person so empowered to deal with your property in all respects as if it were his own, or as if he had for the time being assumed your personality. He may sign your name to any instrument ; he may "bind you to anything he pleases; he may draw money from your bank ; he may impersonate you in all business transactions. In short, as far as business arrangements are concerned, he stands practically and legally for yourself. This is a tremendous power to place in the hands of another, and people should be very careful to whom they assign It. It should never be conferred on any person but one whose honesty is above suspicion, and whose knowledge of business and of men and affairs has been tried and proved.

" Oh, I signed a paper, giving full power of attorney to my lawyer before I went abroad I trusted everything to him, and when I came back practically everything was gone. My business affairs were so complicated that I have not had the money to fight the man I trusted." This was, in brief, the story of one man's wrecked finances, as he told it to me.

Women will often pay out large sums of money, and never think of asking for a receipt, especially if they are dealing with friends or people they know well. Intelligent women, however, ought to know that our government is a good example of how we should do business. It does not doubt President Roosevelt's honesty, and yet he must sign a voucher for his salary, just the same as the cheapest government employee. The justices of the United States Supreme Court, who are considered to be the soul of honor, and are the final arbiters of all great questions, must also sign a receipt for their salaries.

If every child in America had a thorough business training, tens of thousands of promoters, long-headed, cunning schemers, who have thriven on the people's ignorance, would be out of an occupation.

I believe that the business colleges are among the greatest blessings in American civilization to-day, because through their teaching they have been the means of saving thousands of homes, and have made happy and comfortable tens of thousands of people who might otherwise be living in poverty and wretchedness.

'This ignorance of practical business principles is very common among professional men. I know clergymen, journalists, authors, doctors, teachers, men in every profession, who are constantly subjected to serious embarrassment by their incapacity in business matters. Some of them do not know how to interpret the simplest business forms.

Not long ago, a Harvard graduate, occupying a very important position as a teacher, went to the president of a commercial school and asked him to give him some lessons on how to handle money, notes, etc. He said that when he went to his bank and asked them how much money he had there, they laughed at him; and that when a bank draft came to him he did not know what to do with it.

Nothing will stand you in better stead, in the hard, cold practical everyday world, than a good, sound business education. You will find that your success in any trade, occupation, or profession will depend as much on your general knowledge of men and affairs as on your technical training.

No matter what your vocation may be, you must be a business man first, or you will always be placed at a great disadvantage in the practical affairs of life. We cannot entirely ignore the money side of existence any more than we can the food side, and the very foundation of a practical, successful life is the ability to know how to manage the money side effectively.

It is infinitely harder to save money and to invest it wisely than to make it, and, if even the most practical men, men who have had a long training in scientific business methods, find it a difficult thing to hold on to money after they make it, what is likely to happen to people who have had practically no training in business methods?

XIV.

SIZING UP PEOPLE

AFTER Alexander the Great had conquered the Persians he became suddenly very ill. One of his generals sent him a letter saying that his attending physician had resolved to poison him. He read the letter without the slightest sign of emotion, and put it under his pillow. When the physician came and prepared medicine, Alexander said he would not take it just then, but told him to put it where he could reach it, and at the same time gave him the letter from his general. Alexander raised himself on his elbow, and watched the physician's face with the most searching scrutiny, looking into his very soul ; but he did not see in it the slightest evidence of fear or guilt. He immediately reached for the medicine bottle, and, without a word, drank its contents. The amazed physician asked him how he could do that after receiving such a letter. Alexander replied, *"Because you are an honest man."*

Alexander was a remarkable student of human nature. He knew men, and the motives which actuated them. He could read the human heart as an open book.

The art of all arts for the leader is this ability to measure men, to weigh them, to " size them up," to estimate their possibilities, to place them so as to call out their strength and eliminate their weakness.

This is the epitaph which Andrew Carnegie has chosen for himself: "Here lies a man who knew how to get around him men much cleverer than himself."

People wonder how a Morgan, a Harriman, a Ryan, a Wanamaker, can carry on such prodigious enterprises. The secret lies in their ability to project themselves through a mighty system, and to choose men who will fit the places they are put in, men who can carry out their employer's programme to the letter.

Marshall Field was always studying his employees and trying to read their futures. Nothing escaped his keen eye. Even when those about him did not know that he was thinking of them, he was taking their measure at every opportunity. His ability to place men, to weigh and measure them, to pierce all pretense, amounted to genius. When he missed a man from a certain counter, he would often ask his manager what had become of him. When told that he was promoted, he would keep track of him until he missed him again, and then would ask where he was. He always wanted to see how near the man came to his estimate of him. He thus kept track of men of promise in his employ and watched their advancement. In this way, he became an expert in human nature reading.

Mr. Field would sometimes pick out a man for a position the choice of whom his advisers would tell him they thought a mistake; but he was nearly always right, because he had greater power of discernment than the others. He did not pay much attention to the claims of the applicant, or to what he said, because he could see through the surface and measure the real man. He had a wonderful power for taking a man's mental caliber. He could see in which direction his strength lay, and he could see his weak points as few men could.

A man who had been his general manager for many years, once resigned very suddenly to go into business for himself. Without the slightest 'hesitation or concern, Mr. Field called to his office a man whom he had been watching, unknown to the man, for a long time. With very few words, he made him general manager. And so great was his confidence that he had measured the man correctly, that the very next day he sailed for Europe. He did not think it necessary to wait and see how his new manager turned out. He believed he had the right man and that he could trust him. He was not disappointed.

Men who are capable of succeeding in a large way are shrewd enough to know that they do not " know it all," shrewd enough to employ men who are strong where they are weak, to surround themselves with men who have the ability which they lack, who can supplement their weakness and shortcomings with strength and ability. Thus, in their combined power, they make an effective force.

Many men, because of their inability to read human nature, duplicate their own weaknesses in their employees, thus multiplying their chances of failure. Few men are able to see their own weaknesses and limitations, and those who do not, surround themselves with men who have the same weak links in their character, and the result is that their whole institution is weak.

The leader must not only be able to judge others, but he must also be able to read himself, to take an inventory of his own strong points and weak points.

Men who have been elected to high office or to fill very important positions at the head of great concerns because of their recognized ability have often disappointed the expectations of those who placed their hopes in them, simply because they could not read people. They may have been well educated, well posted, strong intellectually, may have had a great deal of general ability; but they lacked the skill to read men, to measure them, to weigh them, to place them where they belonged.

Grant was cut out for a general, a military leader ; but when he got into the White House he felt out of place, he was shorn of his great He was obliged to depend too much upon the advice of friends. The result was that, as President, he did not maintain the high reputation he had made as a general.

If he had the same ability to read politicians and to estimate men for government positions that he had for judging of military ability, he would have made a great President ; but he felt his weakness in the position which he was not fitted by nature to fill, and made the fatal mistake of putting himself into the hands of his friends.

The young man starting out for himself ought to make a study of his power of penetration, of his character-reading ability. He ought to make it a business to study men, to estimate their capabilities and the motives which actuate them. He should scrutinize their actions, watch their tendencies in little things, and learn to read them as an open book.

The involuntary acts and natural manner of a man indicate more than does his studied conversation. The eye cannot lie. It speaks the truth in all languages. It often contradicts the tongue. While the man is trying to deceive you with words, his eyes are telling you the truth; his actions are indicative of the real man, while the tongue may only represent the diplomat, the man who is acting.

A very successful business man in New York, noted for his ability to read men, will sometimes study an applicant for an important position for a long time, talking very little himself, but all the time trying to call the man out, watching every movement, scrutinizing every word, trying to read the motive behind every glance of the eye. His manner, everything, are all letters of the alphabet by which he spells out the real man. I have been in his office when he was measuring a man. It was a great lesson to watch his face as he seemed to read the applicant through and through, weigh him on the scale of his judgment, penetrate to the very marrow of his being, and estimate his capabilities and possibilities to a nicety.

After a few minutes' conversation, and the man had passed out, he would tell me just how large that man was, what he was capable of doing, what his future would be, and what were his limitations. And he seldom makes a mistake. I have never known a man to succeed to any extent when he said there was nothing in him, and I have never known one to turn out badly when he indorsed him without reserve.

We all know heads of business houses who work like slaves, dig and save, and yet do not make much headway, simply because they do not know how to surround themselves with the right men.

Some men seem incapable of projecting system and order through their establishments. They may do their own work well, and then they strike their limitations. They are not good judges of human nature; their discernment is not sharp. They are misled by conversational powers, display of education, and often place a theoretical man where only practical talent could succeed. They are likely to place a man of great refinement, sensitiveness, delicate make-up, in a position where a strong, robust, thick-skinned man is required, where an oversensitive soul will chafe and shrink from the cold, aggressive business methods necessary to effective, efficient management.

People are continually being led into all sorts of unfortunate positions, entangling alliances, and mortifying, embarrassing situations because of their lack of ability to read human nature and to estimate character at a glance. Good people everywhere are being imposed upon and are losing their money in all sorts of foolish investments because of their ignorance of human nature. They are not able to see the rascal, the scoundrel behind the mask. They have not developed the power of discernment, the ability to see the " wolf in sheep's clothing." The knowledge of human nature as a protector of money, of character, as a protector against frauds and imposition is inestimable.

Gullible people are proverbially poor readers of human nature, and hence they are always open to imposition. Oily, cunning promoters are keen observers of human nature, and they can tell very quickly when they strike a good natured, large-hearted professor, scholar, clergyman or artist who knows very little about business matters and who trusts everybody. They know that if they can only get an opportunity they can very quickly make such a man believe almost anything. They know he will be an easy prey to their wiles and their keener knowledge of men.

These promoters would not think of tackling a shrewd, level-headed business man for their nefarious schemes, because he is too keen, too sharp, too good a judge of human nature. Such a man would be likely to penetrate the mask and see the real motive beneath the oily, honeyed words, the smooth seductive manner.

The ability to read people at sight is a great business asset. Expertness in reading human nature is just as valuable to a young lawyer as a knowledge of law; it is as valuable to a physician as a knowledge of medicine. The man who can read human nature, who can" size up" a person quickly, who can arrive at an accurate estimate of character, no matter what his vocation, or profession, has a great advantage over others.

With some men the power to read people a right amounts to an instinct. They look through all pretenses; they tear off all masks. They see the man as he is, his reality, and measure him for what he is worth.

A man possessing this power of character-reading pays little attention to what a person seeking employment may say of himself. He can see for himself. Human nature is to him an open book, while to others it is a sealed book. They do not have the faculty of going back of pretensions. They are largely at the mercy of what he claims for himself, and they are always being duped. They make very poor employers.

I know a popular business man, a very able man in many respects, and one much beloved by everybody who knows him, but he has always been the victim of his ignorance of human nature. He cannot read motives, weigh or estimate the ability of others to do certain things. If an applicant for a position talks well, he immediately jumps to the conclusion that he is a good man for the position, and hires him, usually to be disappointed. He has a great weakness for clergymen who have lost their positions through failing health or for other reasons, and also for ex-teachers and professors. The result is that he has a lot of impractical people about him who know nothing of progressive, scientific business building.

It is an education in itself to form the habit of measuring, weighing, estimating the different people we meet, for in this way we are improving our own powers of observation, sharpening our perspective faculties, improving our judgment. The ability to read human nature is a cultivable quality, and we have a great opportunity in this country, with its conglomerate population, to study the various types of character.

What a wonderful school most of us are in practically all of the time, especially in large cities, where we are constantly coming in contact with strangers! What a chance to become experts in reading human nature, in studying motives !

The face, the eye, the manners, the gestures, the walk, all these are hieroglyphics which, if we can only decipher them, spell out the character. Sometimes a single glance of the eye, when one is unconscious, will give you a glimpse into his innermost soul and reveal secrets which he would never dare to utter with his tongue. The facial expression and the manner, especially when people are off their guard, or unconscious that they are being watched, are great revealers of character.

You will find, as you become an expert in face study, in reading character, human nature, that you will develop marvelous skill in seeing things which you never noticed before. You will be able to protect yourself from the promoter, the insinuating man who is trying to persuade you into something which may not be to your benefit, but which will be to his. You will be able to discriminate between friendship and duplicity. You will be able to protect yourself from a thousand annoyances and embarrassments and humiliations which might cripple your career.

How many people are living in poverty, are wretched, homeless to-day because they could not read human nature and were robbed of their property and their rights !

To discern the difference between the false and the true, to place the right values upon men, to emphasize the right thing in them, to discriminate between the genuine and the pretended, is an accomplishment which may be worth infinitely more to you than a college education without this practical power, and may make all the difference to you between success and failure, happiness and misery.

XV.

DOES THE WORLD OWE YOU A LIVING?

A FIFTEEN-YEAR-OLD bell boy, was arrested in Cleveland, for stealing eight dollars. When asked in court why he stole, he said "Because the world owes me a living." No doubt the youth had heard this many times from older lips.

When the armies of Louis XIV. were devastated in Flanders, the monarch exclaimed: " Has God forgotten all that I have done for him? " A vast number of people seem to think that God and the world are under great obligations to them, and that the world owes them a living without any return service from them. Not long ago I heard a young woman say that she did not consider that she owed the world anything, that she was thrust into it without being consulted, that she proposed to get out of it what she could with as little effort as possible, and that she did not feel under the slight- est obligation to the past.

Did you ever think, my idle friend, what you really owe the world for the privilege of living in it? Did you ever think that all the civilizations of the globe have been working for you through all the ages up to the present moment, and that you are reaping the harvest of all the hard-working, sacrificing, suffering, drudging sowers that have preceded you?

Can you look the workers of the world in the face and tell them that you intend to have all the benefits of their labor, to enjoy all the good things of the world without doing anything to compensate for them?

The man who does not feel his heart throb with gratitude every day of his life for being born in the very golden age of the world, and who does not feel that he owes a tremendous debt to the past, to all the people who have struggled and striven and sacrificed before him, is not made of the right kind of stuff. In other words, he is not a man, and he ought to be treated as a drone, a thief of other men's labors.

Everything that has gone before you, enters into your life and time. You enjoy the sum of all the past every moment of your life. Think of the untold thousands who have laid down their lives to make possible the comforts, the blessings, and the immunities you now enjoy. Think of the rivers of blood that have been spilt, of the thousands who have perished or lived in the misery of prison and dungeon to purchase the liberties of speech and freedom of action which you enjoy to-day.

How many lives have been lived in solitude and misery in order to develop sciences which are to-day beacon lights of the world! And think what multitudes of people are engaged in producing, manufacturing and forwarding your clothing, your furniture, your food, the tropical fruits on your table, the foreign textiles, the bric-a-brac, and all the things which come from foreign lands to minister to your comfort and convenience.

You buy an orange on the street for two or three cents, but did you ever think of what it has cost to bring it to you? Did you ever think of the number of people who have aided in its production and its transportation so that you might buy it for a few pennies ?

You get a yard of cotton cloth for ten cents ; but did you ever think of the toil and the hardships of the poor people in the South, of the operatives in the mill, the packers, shippers, and clerks who have handled and rehandled, and shipped it by steamship and railroad that you might buy it for a song?

Suppose these people who say that they owe the world nothing were obliged to make all the comforts and luxuries they enjoy! How long would it take them to produce even a lead pencil, a sheet of writing paper, a jackknife, a pair of spectacles, a pair of shoes, or a suit of clothes, representing an untold amount of drudgery and sacrifice? There is toil, struggle, and sacrifice in everything you purchase, everything you enjoy. How many thousands of people have worked like slaves to make it even possible for you to ride on a railroad or on a steamship, and how many lives have been sacrificed in order to reach the perfection and safety attained by modern trains and steamers, and to enable you to enjoy the comforts and luxuries which they provide!

Wherever you go, tens of thousands of people have been preparing the way and getting things ready, guarding against danger, saving you trouble and drudgery; and yet you say that you do not consider yourself in debt to the world.

If all the workers and all the wealth of the world to-day had been employed for thousands of years for your special benefit, to prepare for your reception upon the earth, they could not have provided the comforts, the conveniences, the facilities, the immunities, the luxuries which you found waiting for you when you were born, and for which you gave not even a penny or a thought, and yet you say that the world owes you this and the other, and that you owe it nothing!

Did you ever think, my idle friend, that there are some things which are not purchasable with money? Do not deceive yourself by thinking that you will get something for nothing. All the laws of the universe are fighting such a theory. You must open an account with the world personally. No one else can pay the debt you owe. Whatever money or advantages your father or any one else gets by his own efforts nature has stamped "untransferable." The law of the universe recognizes only one legal tender, and that is, personal service.

Whatever you get of real value you must pay for. The things that are done for you are delusions. You are a personal debtor to the world. When you were born, civilization opened an account with you. On one side of the ledger you find: " John Smith, debtor to all the past ages for the sum total of the results of the toil of the men and the women who have lived and toiled before him. Debtor to the privations, the sufferings, and the sacrifices of those who have bought freedom from bondage, immunity from slavery, emancipation from drudgery." You are debtor to all the inventions that have ameliorated the hard conditions of mankind and which have emancipated you from the same hard drudgery and stern conditions, the same narrow, limited life of your prehistoric ancestors.

Who are you, Mr. Idler, that you claim a living from the world, when you have not earned the clothing you have on your back or the shelter which covers your head? Why should tens of thousands of people drudge and endure hardships and privations to produce all of the useful things, the beautiful things, the luxuries for you to enjoy without effort?

You say the world owes you a living. What if the sheep should refuse to furnish its wool to cover your lazy back, the earth refuse to produce the crops to fill your lazy stomach, the army of laborers refuse to let you take all the good things out of the world's great granary without putting anything back? What would become of you who have never lifted your finger to learn a trade or to prepare yourself for a career, or to do work of any kind, if an edict were to come from the skies that would force you henceforth to do your share of the world's work or starve?

Is he not a thief, an enemy of civilization who thrusts his arm into the great world's storehouse, pulling out all the good things he wishes and refusing to put anything back in exchange ?

We hear a great deal about indiscriminate giving making paupers; but what shall we say about the giving of fortunes to youth who have never been taught that they should give anything in return for all they receive ?

What are the chances of growth in character, in sturdy manhood, for the boy who knows that a fortune is waiting for him when he is twenty-one, and who is told every day that his father is rich and that he is a fool to work; that he should just make a business of having a good time ? What are the chances of his developing a rugged, sturdy independence, resourcefulness, originality, inventiveness, and all the other qualities that make for vigorous manhood? It is cruel, little less than criminal, to leave vast fortunes to youth without stamina of character, a superb, practical training, or the experience or wisdom to use them wisely.

Things are so arranged in this world that happiness as a profession must ever be a failure. It cannot be found by seeking. It is reflex action. It is incidental; a product which comes from doing noble things. It is impossible for a person to be really happy by making pleasure a profession.

No idle life can produce a real man. A life of luxury calls out only the effeminate, destructive qualities. The creative forces are developed only by stern endeavor to better one's condition in the world. No wealth or efforts of the parents can bring the latent energies out in the son which make for sturdy manhood. He must work out his problem himself. It can never be done for him.

How little Harry Thaw's parents realized the cruelty of bringing their son up in idleness, without a trade or a profession, helpless to earn his own living in case of necessity! One would think they would have learned wisdom from the tens of thousands of lessons which ruined lives have taught ; that there is no getting around God's fiat, no evading the law, that work, exercise of faculty, self-effort are the only things that will develop a real man.

The Creator has put an enormous penalty upon idleness the penalty of weakness, of deterioration, of destruction, of annihilation. "Use or lose" is Nature's edict.

The idle man is like an idle machine. It destroys itself very quickly. A score of enemies are in readiness to attack anything as soon as it is at rest. Rust, decay, and all sorts of disintegrating processes start in a man just as soon as he becomes idle. Self-destruction begins in the mind the moment it ceases to work. There is no power in heaven or on earth that can save an idle brain from deterioration, no power that can make a man strong and vigorous unless he obeys the natural laws of his life, written in his very constitution. Work, steady, persistent, with a purpose, with zeal, with enthusiasm, with a love for it, is the only thing that can save a man from the disgrace of being a nobody. Work is the inexorable law of growth. There is no getting away from it.

The time will come when an able-bodied man who has the audacity, the presumption, to try to get all the good things out of the world and give nothing in return will be looked upon as a monstrosity, an enemy to civilization, and will be ostracized by all decent people.

The youth who thinks he is going to go through this world on what somebody else has produced or done, and still develop into the highest type of a man, is attempting to fight against his Maker. The very laws of the universe have made it forever impossible. Leave this vast, living, complicated machine idle, if you will, try to divert it to some other use, try to make a pleasure machine out of it when it was intended for a work machine, but all nature protests.

One of the most demoralizing features of our American civilization to-day is found in the influence of the idle rich great human drones, who refuse to work, but who demand the best products of other men's labor and brains.

I have heard rich fathers boast that necessity was the spur which made men of them, which gave them the foresight, the stamina, the shrewdness, the creative power, the ability necessary to make and protect their fortune; and yet they turn right around and leave a fortune to a son, which is likely to take away his energy, to take the spring out of his ambition, to rob him of the zest, the enthusiasm which can only come from the exercise of earnest, honest effort.

No man is so rich, no matter how honestly he got his money, as to be able to confer immunity from work upon his offspring. The very nature of things, the eternal law of the universe has made it forever impossible for you to transfer the stamina, the vigorous manhood, the stability, the character, everything that is of real value which you have gained in your struggle to get on in the world, to your son or daughter. Your offspring owes a debt to civilization which goes back of the parent. It is a debt which can only be wiped out by the individual. It cannot be discharged by proxy. Personal effort is the condition of the child's development. It is the inevitable price of manhood.

No, there are some things you rich fathers cannot do for your boy. There is a law of nature which prohibits it, an omnipotent principle which protests against it.

If a phrenologist should examine the heads of the idle, grown-up sons of rich men, he would find very marked deficiencies, an underdevelopment of nearly all of the qualities which make strong men. He would usually find selfishness very largely developed; self-reliance, originality, inventiveness, resourcefulness, and all the other qualities which are drawn out and strengthened only by self-help and the struggle to make one's way in the world, little developed.

If he should compare them with the heads of their self-made fathers, he would find very marked inferiority, so marked that there would apparently be no relationship between the owners of the heads.

The contrast would be as great as that between the hard, tough, firm fiber of the mountain oak and the fiber of the soft, spongy sapling which never struggled with the storm and tempest because sheltered by surrounding trees.

How little a father realizes that it is one of the cruelest things he could do to his boy to practically rob him of the opportunity of making a real man of himself, of developing qualities which make strength, power, which build vigorous, stalwart manhood!

There is something about the actual making of one's way in the world, of burning behind one all bridges which others have built, throwing away all crutches and refusing to lean, to be boosted, refusing all assistance and standing erect upon one's own feet, thinking his own thoughts, fighting his own battles, bringing out his own latent possibilities by actual exercise, bringing into action every bit of one's inventiveness, resourcefulness, ingenuity and originality, tact, that makes a man strong, vigorous, and stalwart, which indicates that this is the normal life of a man, the only life which can develop the true man.

The army of inefficient the namby-pambies, the dressed-up nobodies, with soft hands and softer heads, who are expert only in saying "silly nothings to silly women," or in the practice of some useless fad, the " amount-to-nothings " everywhere, ought to convince you that there is no way of getting something for nothing.

If you will not do a man's work, if you will not pay a man's price for manhood, you will be only an apology for a man. Of course, you can live the life of the idle if you will. If you are the son of a foolish rich father, no one may be able to hinder you ; but you must take the idler's reward. You must go through life branded with the shame, labeled with the weakness, marked with the deformities of idleness. You must pay the penalty of your choice and be a nobody.

XVI.

WHAT HAS LUCK DONE FOR YOU?

FORTUNE brings in some boats that are not steer'd." People may say what they will about there not being any such thing as "luck," or "chance," but we must all admit there is such a thing. We must all concede that things over which a man has no control, unforeseen happenings, or events with which he has had nothing to do and on which he had not calculated, often change the whole course of his career. Good positions do not always come by merit, or as the result of one's own direct efforts. It is now a poor laboring man or washerwoman who falls heir to a fortune by the death of some relative; or, again it is a poor girl who is suddenly raised to wealth and what the world calls high position by marrying a man of rank or fortune.

Every schoolboy knows that there is a great advantage in being in the right place in just the nick of time, and that being there is often a matter of chance. Men are constantly being moved up into positions which they did not get wholly by merit. Their elevation is due, haps, to a railroad accident, a stroke of paralysis, or the death of men in high places. We had a striking instance of this, recently, in the death of two presidents of the Long Island Railroad within a few months, which led to unexpected promotions. Everyone knows that men are constantly being put at the head of large concerns because of kinship with the owners of the business, when perhaps a score of those who are working in the establishments, at the time, are much better fitted to fill the positions.

But, after all, who will be foolish enough to say that man is the toy of chance, or that true success is the result of accident or fate?

No luck is not God's price for success, nor does He dicker with men. When we consider the few who owe fortune or position to accident or luck, in comparison with the masses who have to fight every inch of the way to their own loaves, what are they, in reality, but the exceptions to the rule that *character*, merit not fate, or luck, or any other bogy of the imagination controls the destinies of men? The only luck that plays any great part in a man's life is that which inheres in a stout heart, a willing hand, and an alert brain.

What has chance ever done in the world? Has it invented a telegraph or telephone? Has it laid an ocean cable ? Has it built steamships, or established universities, asylums, or hospitals? Has it tunneled mountains, built bridges, or brought miracles out of the soil?

What did luck have to do with making the career of Washington, of Lincoln, of Daniel Webster, of Henry Clay, of Grant, of Garfield, or of Elihu Root? Did it help Edison or Marconi with his inventions? Did it have anything to do with the making of the fortunes of our great merchant princes? Do such men as John Wanamaker, Robert Ogden, or Marshall Field owe their success to luck?

Many a man has tried to justify his failure on the ground that he was doomed by the cards which fate dealt him, that he must pick them up and play the game, and that no effort, however great, on his part, could materially change the result. But, my young friend, the fate that deals your cards is in the main your own resolution. The result of the game does not rest with fate or destiny, but with you. You will take the trick if you have the superior energy, ability, and determination requisite to take it. You have the power within yourself to change the value of the cards which, you say, fate has dealt you. The game depends upon your training, upon the way you are disciplined to seize and use your opportunities, and upon your ability to put grit in the place of superior advantages.

Just because circumstances sometimes give clients to lawyers and patients to physicians, put commonplace clergymen in uncommon pulpits, and place the sons of the rich at the head of great corporations even when they have only average ability and scarcely any experience, while poor youths with greater ability, and more experience, often have to fight their way for years to obtain ordinary situations, are you justified in starting out without a chart or in leaving a place for luck in your programme? What would you think of a captain of a great liner who would start out to sea without any port in view, and trust to luck to land his precious cargo safely?

Did you ever know of a strong young man making out his life-programme and depending upon chance to carry out any part of it ? Men who depend upon luck do not think it worth while to make a thorough preparation for success. They are not willing to pay the regular price for it. They are looking for bargains. They are hunting for short cuts to success.

We hear a great deal about "Roosevelt's luck "; but what would it have availed him if he was not ready for the opportunity when it came if he had not trained himself through years of persistent drill to grasp it if he had not been prepared to make the best use of it?

I have never known a man to amount to much until he cut out of his vocabulary such words as " good luck " and " bad luck," and from his life-maxims all the " I can't " words and the I can't " philosophy. There is no word in the English language more misused and abused than " luck." More people have excused themselves for poor work and mean, stingy, poverty-stricken careers, by saying " luck was against them " than by any other plea.

That door ahead of you, young man, is probably closed because you have closed it closed it by lack of training ; by a lack of ambition, energy, and push. While, perhaps, you have been waiting for luck to open it, a pluckier, grittier fellow has stepped in ahead of you and opened it himself. Power gravitates to the man who knows how. " Luck is the tide, nothing more. The strong man rows with it if it makes toward his port; he rows against it if it flows the other way."

When Governor John A. Johnson, of Minnesota, was asked, " How do you account for your success?" he answered, simply, "I just tried to make good." You will find, nine hundred and ninety-nine times out of a thousand, that the man who tries to make good is the " lucky man." Young Johnson had to fight against poverty, heredity and environment everything that could be put forward as an excuse for " bad luck," or " no chance," yet in his hard battle with fate he never once faltered, or whined, or complained that luck was against him.

One of the most unfortunate delusions that ever found its way into a youth's brain is that there is some force or power outside of himself that will, in some mysterious way, and with very little effort on his part, lift him into a position of comfort and luxury. I never knew any one who followed the ignis fatuus, luck who did not follow it to his ruin. " Good luck " follows good sense, good judgment, good health, a gritty determination, a lofty ambition, and downright hard work.

When you see horses in a race, you know perfectly well that the one in the lead is ahead because he has run faster than the others, and you would not have much sympathy for the horse behind if he should bemoan his fate and declare that the horse ahead had a snap! When you see any one doing better than you are doing under similar circumstances, just say to yourself, "There must be some reason for it. There is a secret back of it, and I must find it out." Do not try to ease your conscience or lull your ambition by pleading " hard luck" for yourself, or good fortune for another.

Napoleon said that " God is always on the side of the strongest battalions. He is always on the side of the best prepared, the best trained, the most vigilant, the pluckiest, and the most determined. If we should examine the career of most men who are called lucky, we should find that their success has its roots far back in the past, and has drawn its nourishment from many a battle in the struggle for supremacy over poverty and opposition. We should probably find that the " lucky " man is a closer thinker than the " unlucky " man, that he has a finer judgment, that he has more system and order; that his brain acts more definitely and concisely, that he thinks more logically, more vigorously, and that he is more practical. Life is not a game of chance. The Creator did not put us where we would be the sport of circumstances, to be tossed about by a cruel fate, regardless of our own efforts.

XVII.

SUCCESS WITH A FLAW

JUST now the American people are receiving some painful lessons in practical ethics," said President Nicholas Murray Butler, recently. " They are having brought home to them, with severe emphasis, the distinction between character and reputation. ... Of late we have been watching reputations melt away like snow before the sun. . . . Put bluntly, the situation which confronts the American people to-day is due to the lack of moral principle."

Never before in the history of our country have the American people received a greater shock to their faith in human nature than during the past year, by the exposure of the diabolical methods practised by men in high places upon an admiring and unsuspecting people.

Every little while the public press throws X-rays upon the characters of men who have long stood high and spotless in the public eye, and have been looked up to as models of manhood, men of honorable achievement revealing great ugly stains of dishonor, which, like the blood spot on Lady Macbeth's hands, all the oceans of the globe cannot wash out.

A tiny flaw sometimes cuts the value of an otherwise thousand-dollar diamond down to fifty dollars or less. The defect is not noticeable to the average person. It is only the fatal magnifying glass that will detect it, and yet its presence is a perpetual menace to the commercial value of the stone. A great many human diamonds which, a little while ago, were thought to be flawless brilliants of the first water, and which dazzled the financial and social world, when the microscope of official scrutiny was turned upon them, were found to contain great ugly flaws.

A United States senator, seventy years of age, was recently sentenced to serve a term in prison, besides paying a fine, for his connection with great land frauds. Still another senator and several representatives have been indicted for crooked work in connection with their exalted positions. Congressmen have been convicted of land frauds and army officers of peculation. The exposure of post office contracts and the notorious " cotton statistics leak," not long ago, showed that minor officials had sold themselves to manufacturers and Wall Street brokers.

Think of the men at the head of great public trusts juggling with sacred funds, not only taking for themselves, from the hard earned savings of the poor, salaries two or three times as great as that of the President of the United States, but also giving enormous salaries to a large number of their relatives out of these same sacred funds of those who have struggled for years to make possible a better condition for those who should survive them ! Think of their paying out hundreds of thousands of dollars for secret services of a suspicious nature, and using trust funds to effect stock manipulations for private gain!

Was there ever before such a shameful story spread before Americans? Were people ever before so mercilessly betrayed by men they looked up to, admired, and implicitly trusted? Never before has there been such colossal stealing carried on so brazenly and openly by men in high positions.

Some of these men, when they appeared in public a year ago, were applauded to the echo. Wherever they went they were followed by admiring crowds. Some months ago I saw one of them, a man who has been for many years a great public favorite, at a reception in the White House. He was pointed out by guests, and seemed to attract almost as much attention as the President himself. People seemed to regard it as a great honor to be introduced to him. Now he would hardly dare to appear before an audience for fear of being hissed.

What a humiliation for those whose names have been household words for a quarter of a century or more to be asked to withdraw from trusteeships or directorships in institutions which perhaps worked for years to secure these men, on account of their great influence, and high reputations.

What is there left worth living for when a man has lost the finest, the most sacred thing in him, and when he has forfeited the confidence and respect of his fellow men? Is there any quality which inheres in dollars that can compensate for such a loss? Is there any thing which ought to be held more precious than honor or more sacred than the esteem and confidence of friends and acquaintances?

The man who has nothing which he holds dearer than money or some material advantage is not a man. The brute has not been educated out of him. The abler a man and the more money he has, the more we despise him if he has gotten that money dishonestly, because of the tremendous contrast between what he has done and what he might have done.

What the world demands of you, whatever your career, whether you make money or lose it, whether you are rich or poor, is that you be a man. It is the man that gives value to achievement. You cannot afford success with a flaw in it. You cannot afford to have people say of you, " Mr. Blank has made money, but there is a stain on it. It is smirched. It has cost him too much. He exchanged his manhood for it.

" Every human being has it within his power to keep the foundation under him his manhood absolutely secure under all circumstances. Nothing can shake that but himself. The citadel can never be taken until he himself surrenders the keys. Calumny, detraction, slander, or monetary failure cannot touch this sacred thing.

Every man, whether in private or public life, should so carry himself before the world that he will show in his very face and manner that there is something within him not for sale something so sacred that he would regard the slightest attempt to debauch it as an unpardonable insult. He should so carry himself that no one would even dare to suggest that he could be bought or bribed.

Who was so corrupt during the Civil War that he would have dared to attempt to bribe Abraham Lincoln? There was something in that face that would have cowed the hardest character. Who would be bold enough to presume to bribe our present President?

Many a one has failed because he was not a man before he was a merchant, or a lawyer, or a manufacturer, or a statesman because character was not the dominating influence in his life. If you are not a man first if there is not a man behind your book, behind your sermon, behind your law brief, or your business transaction if you are not larger than the money you make, the world will expose and despise your pretense and discount your success; history will cover up your memory no matter how much money you may leave.

That is the lesson of the startling disclosures of late. These men whose reputations have melted away so rapidly men who have had such a drop in the public regard were not real men to start with. There were flaws in their character foundations, and the superstructures of their achievement have fallen before the flood of public indignation. Those criminals in high places are beginning to realize that no smartness, brilliancy, genius, scheming, long-headed cunning, bluffing, or pretense can take the place of manhood or be a substitute for personal integrity.

There are men in New York, to-day, whose names have been a power, who would give every dollar they have for a clean record if they could wipe off all their underhanded, questionable methods from the slate and start anew; but there is no way to buy a good name. It is above riches, and beyond the price of rubies.

How many men there are, to-day, in high positions who are in perpetual terror lest something should happen to expose the real facts of their lives something which would pierce their masks and reveal them in their true light. How must a man feel who is conscious that he is walking all the time on the thin crust of a volcano which is liable to open at any moment and swallow him?

There is one thing no money or influence can buy; that is, the heart's approval of a wrong deed or a questionable transaction. It will be bobbing up all along the future to remind you of your theft, of your dishonesty, or of your unfair advantage. It will take the edge off your enjoyment. It will appear, like Banquo's ghost, at every feast to which you sit down.

Methinks that some of the men who have been exposed recently must have had strange dreams and horrid nightmares during their sleep, when the ghosts of the poor people whom they have wronged appeared to them and haunted their rest. Methinks they must have had strange visions as these sacred dollars intended for widows and orphans slipped through their fingers for luxuries and amusements dollars which had been wrung out of the lives of those who trusted them.

What a pitiable picture those great financial giants made, under investigation in courts of inquiry, squirming, ducking, dodging, and re- sorting to all sorts of ingenuity to avoid telling the exact truth to keep from uncovering their tracks or exposing their crooked methods ! No man has a right to put himself in a position where he has to cover up anything or where he must be afraid head, look his kind in the face without wincing, and defy the world.

A man went to President Roosevelt, before the last presidential election, and told him that someone had unearthed a letter of his which would be extremely damaging to his canvass were it made public, and that, with a little diplomacy, the damaging part of the letter could be suppressed. After listening to the man, the great President said, " I have never written a letter which I am afraid to have published. Let them print the letter, the whole of it. I have nothing to conceal. I am not afraid to face anything I have ever done.

How many of our public men dare take that attitude?

Isn't it a disgrace to this fair land that there are men in our Senate and House of Representatives, and in almost every legislature, whose whose honor there is a price?

If there is anything which a man in a responsible position ought to prize, it is the esteem of the young men who look up to him as their idol or hero. Is it strange, when our youth find their idols smashed, and their heroes betraying them, that their ideals should become blurred and twisted? Is it strange that they should ignore the old-fashioned methods of slow fortune-making when they see the smooth, oily, diplomatic schemers getting rich in a few months, and young men who were mere clerks a year ago, now riding in costly automobiles, giving expensive entertainments, and living in fine houses? Why should they not catch the spirit, and try to do the same thing themselves?

You wrongdoers in high places, 'if you should live as long as Methuselah, should devote every minute of the balance of your lives to doing good, and should give every farthing of your wealth to charity, you could not repair the damage you have done in crushing the ideals of these tens of thousands of youths who have looked up to you as their models of successful men. How can you escape responsibility for the crookedness which may be repeated in their lives when they shall come to fill these high positions which you now hold? They thought that square dealing, honesty, and integrity had been the secrets of your success, and now they see that it was won by your smooth, oily, cunning dishonesty your ability to deceive, to cover your tracks, and to live a double life. Who but yourselves will be responsible for the cracks in their characters which may come from the terrible shaking of their confidence in humanity?

But, young men, don't lose your faith in humanity don't let your fallen idols shake your faith in your fellow men for the great majority of people are honest. Let these terrible examples that have recently been held up to you make you all the more determined to build your own superstructure on the eternal rock of right and justice. Let the man in you stand out so boldly in every transaction that the deed, or task you do, however great, will look insignificant in comparison. Get what you can and keep your own good name not a penny more. A dollar more than that would make your whole fortune valueless. If there is a pitiable sight in the world, it is that of a man with the executive ability, sagacity, and foresight, to make a clean fortune, yet using his energies and abilities in making a dirty one a fortune which denounces and condemns him, and is a perpetual disgrace to himself and his family.

The right ought to thunder so loudly in a man's ears, no matter what the business or transaction in which he is engaged, that he cannot hear the wrong or baser suggestion.

Men have two kinds of ambition: one for dollar-making, the other for life-making. Some turn all their ability, education, health, and energy toward the first of these dollar-making and call the result success. Others turn them toward the second into character, usefulness, helpfulness, life-making and the world sometimes calls them failures; but history calls them successes. No price is too great to pay for an untarnished name.

The highest service you can ever render the world, the greatest thing you can ever do, is to make yourself the largest, completest, and squarest man possible. There is no other fame like that no achievement like that.

XVIII.

GETTING AWAY FROM POVERTY

THOSE who have the misfortune to be rich men's sons are heavily weighted in the race," says Andrew Carnegie. " The vast majority of rich men's sons are unable to resist the temptations to which wealth subjects them, and they sink to unworthy lives. It is not from this class that the poor beginner has rivalry to fear. The partner's sons will never trouble you [the poor boys, much, but look out that some boys poorer, much poorer, than yourselves, whose parents cannot afford to give them any schooling, do not challenge you at the post and pass you at the grandstand. Look out for the boy who has to plunge into work directly from the common school, and who begins by sweeping out the office. He is the probable dark horse that will take all the money and win all the applause."

The struggle to get away from poverty has been a great man-developer. Had every human being been born with a silver spoon in his mouth had there been no necessity put upon him to work the race would still be in its infancy. Had everybody in this country been born wealthy, ours would be one of the dark ages. The vast resources of our land would still be undeveloped, the gold would still be in the mines, and our great cities would still be in the forest and the quarry. Civilization owes more to the perpetual struggle of man to get away from poverty than to anything else. We are so constituted that we make our greatest efforts and do our best work while struggling to attain that for which the heart longs. It is practically impossible for most people to make their utmost exertions with- out imperative necessity for it. It is the constant necessity to improve his condition that has urged man onward and developed the stamina and sterling character of the whole race. History abounds in stories of failures of men who started with wealth; and, on the other hand, it is illuminated with examples of those who owe everything to the spur of necessity.

A glance at the history of our own country will show that the vast majority of our successful men in every field were poor boys at the start. Benjamin Franklin, Alexander Hamilton, Andrew Jackson, Henry Clay, Daniel Webster, Abraham Lincoln, Horace Mann, George Peabody, Ulysses S. Grant, James A. Garfield to mention but a few of the great names of past generations rose to distinction from an iron environment and direst poverty. Our most useful and successful men of to-day have, also, been evolved from the school of want and stern necessity. Our great merchants, railroad presidents, university presidents and professors, inventors, scientists, manufacturers, statesmen men in every line of human activity have for the most part, been pushed forward by the goad of necessity, and led onward by the desire to make the most of themselves.

A youth, born and bred in the midst of luxury, who has always leaned upon others, who has never been obliged to fight his way up to his own loaf, and who has been coddled from his infancy, rarely develops great stamina or staying power. He is like the weak sapling in the forest compared with the giant oak which has fought every inch of its way up from the acorn by struggling with storms and tempasts.

Power is the result of force overcome. The giant is made strong in wrestling with difficulties. It is impossible for one who does not have to struggle and to fight obstacles to develop fiber or stamina. To live without trial is to die but half a man."

Strength of character is a thing which must be wrung out of obstacles overcome. Life is a great gymnasium, and no man who sits in a chair and watches the parallel bars and other apparatus ever develops muscles or endurance. A father, by exercising for his son, while he sits down, will never develop his muscle. The son will be a weakling until he uses the dumb-bells and pulley weights himself. How many fathers try to do the exercises for their boys, while they sit on soft benches or easy chairs, watching the process! And still those fathers wonder that their boys come out of the gymnasium weak, with as soft and flabby muscles as they had when they entered.

Isn't it strange that so many successful men who take pride in having made themselves, and consider it the most fortunate thing in the world that they were thrown upon their own resources and were obliged to develop their independence and stamina and self-reliance, should work so hard to keep their children from having the same experience? Isn't it strange that they should provide crutches so that it will be all the more difficult for them to walk alone? that they should take away the strongest possible motive for the development of power by making it unnecessary for them to strive, by providing for every want and guarding them on all sides by wealth?

A famous artist, who was asked if he thought a young man who was studying with him would make a great painter, replied, " No, never: He has an income of six thousand pounds a year." This artist knew how the great struggle against thwarting difficulties brings out power, and how hard it is to develop a strong, manly fiber in the sunshine of wealth.

How many young immigrants have come to this country uneducated, ignorant of our language, friendless and penniless, and yet have risen to positions of distinction and wealth, putting to shame tens of thousands of nativeborn youths who possessed every advantage of wealth, education, and opportunity, but who have never been heard from!

I have in mind a young man of this class who came to this country a comparatively short time ago, but who has already risen to a very important position wholly unaided. He is a remarkable example of a self-educated self-trained, self-disciplined man; and, in the persistent process of his development he has evolved a very strong, positive, aggressive character. He has brought out his latent powers and strengthened his weaker faculties. He has pruned out of his mentality and habits those things which would embarrass and hinder his progress, and has gained such a strong momentum that there seems to be scarcely any limits to what he is likely to become. His is an inspiring example of the possibilities of manhood in America, one which explodes all excuses of the poor boy and girl who think they have absolutely no chance to get up in the world.

I am no advocate of the blessings of poverty, considered as a finality. Poverty is of no value except as a vantage ground for a starting point. It is only good as is the apparatus in the gymnasium to develop the man. In itself it is a curse slavery but it is the great thing to get away from ; and it is the getting away from it if honestly and conscientiously done that calls out the man, that develops the human giant.

We did not always see, at the time, that what we got incidentally on the way up from poverty was infinitely better and more precious than the thing we were aiming for a living, a competence; that the development of a strong man in the mighty struggle with necessity was a thousand times more valuable than the living, the money, or the property gained.

Grover Cleveland, who was once a poor clerk at a salary of fifty dollars a year, in speaking of poverty as a developer, says: " There is surely no development of mental traits, and no stimulation of the forces of true manhood so thorough and so imperiously effective as those produced by the combination of well-regulated ambition with the healthful rigors of poverty."

It is the student who has to struggle hardest to obtain an education that gets the most discipline and good out of it. Boys who are " born scholars," and who only need to read a lesson over to know it and to be able to pass an examination upon it, do not derive half so much from their college course as do those who have to fight hard for everything they get. It is not, as a rule, the youth who has a regular income and every want supplied by indulgent parents who makes the most of his opportunities at college, but the one who has to work his way through, who has to toil in college and out to make his expenses, or else go without an education.

What would the average youth do if he were not compelled by necessity to work if he were not obliged to exert himself in order to get the thing he wants? If he already has all he wants, why should he struggle for more? Not one in ten thousand would go through the struggle with poverty the wrestling with necessity just to produce character and make himself a stronger man, but he would do it for selfish reasons to satisfy his ambition and get that which he longs for for himself and those he loves.

" I'm not wasting my sympathy on the children of the poor," says U. S. Senator J. P. Dolliver, once a poor boy himself. " What little sympathy I have I will give to the children of the rich. If you have one hundred thousand dollars, and give it to a boy to start him out in life, he doesn't start. I suggest keeping that hundred thousand and that boy apart; it will be better for the boy. The cabin where Abraham Lincoln was born did not shelter the childhood of a king, but something better than a king *a man.*"

The boy who is conscious that he has a fortune awaiting him says to himself, " What is the use of getting up early in the morning and working one's life out? I have money enough coming to me to take care of me as long as I live." So he turns over and takes another nap, while the boy who has nothing in the world but his own self to depend upon feels the spur of necessity forcing him out of bed in the morning. He knows there is no other way open for him but the way of struggle. He has nobody to lean on nobody to help him. He knows that it is a question either of being a nobody or getting up and hustling for dear life.

Thus, shrewd Nature, in making man get that which he wants most by the way of necessity, brings about her great ends of civilization and character-development of the race. The money, the property, the position are small things in comparison with the man she is after.

What price will Nature not pay for a man ? She will put him through the hardest school of discipline, and train him for years in the great university of experience, in order to perfect her work. The mere money or property the man gets on the way is only incidental. Nature is after the man. She does not care a fig for the money, in comparison; but she will pay any price for a human giant.